millennial ephemera

avi sato

springwaterspress

Poems.

Print ISBN 978-1-7770713-4-9
Digital ISBN 978-0-9877194-1-6

Issued simultaneously in print and electronic formats.

Published in Canada.

for Jean and Bob

who inspired me to taste

the music of language's afterlife

行く春や

鳥啼き魚の

目は泪

spring passes
birds mourn as fish weep
with tearful eyes

Matsuo Bashō

mind

darkness absorbs thoughts

as each follows nature

drifting second to second

embodiment of light

when first it connects

through grayscale's moderate depths

deceptive differentiations

from monochrome ink

limits cease to distinguish

hope existing no longer

if ever it had

memory unclear

its presence forgotten

how to regain what may never have been

purity

not truth

simple absence of form

constraints ceasing to mold

soul walls rendered metaphysic

dust of ages

in darkness' thoroughness

tacit creativity

surrenders to absence

self only thought exercises

emotion repetition's shadow

mirror of other selves

themselves limitless echoes

freedom's searches become discouraged

without light

peaceful possibilities extinguish

spirits' dreams

light escapes

sunrays create shadows

beneath peaks of interest

brightness overwhelms

moments of inadequacy

equality crushed by geologic plates

movement unseen

density shifted

underfoot thoughts collapse

within quakes of conscience

faults' cracks appearing

no longer between convenient footpath stones

disintegrate soul components

few become many

now myriad

sparks' gathering remains possible

only moments longer

flourishing improbable

survival the new goal

one is not

cohesion requires black holes of integrity

horizons' fears

attract moments of clarity

light escapes

leaves not darkness

only absence

revision

imagined droplets of image

condense to ceramic frameworks

shattering within rice paper memories

decimated by repetition

obsessive expectation of unchanging circumstance

giving ground to spontaneous fiction

inconsequential truth appears

as mashup of deceit

self built on lies

told without recognition

perception refocused

through mistaken lenses

purchased on transcendental credit

delivered overnight

on condition of final sale

mind adjusts to remember nonevents

erasing significance

replacing history with papier-mâché pasts

novel descriptions spring

from tectonic underpinnings

no longer unexpected

revision ceasing as examination precondition

become concrete backstory

existence arisen from foundations of quicksand

inverted minefields open lakes of disguise

tomorrow floats beyond untold depths' horizon

screen

dear muse

do not simply inspire thought

compel digits

to caress loving sculptures

from the merest touch

reform pixels

in the image of spoken beauty

tear hate from synapse

and build it

in memory of unuttered lies

become me

in flickered half-awareness

beneath covers

clothe passive voices

with newly sacred icons

let active thought

be derived

within first reading's meetup

between fingertips' scrolling

and eyes' briefest escape

from notifications

drawing me to worship

their immediacies' deities

compose in me

lyrics beyond communication

instantiate newly objectified realities

from my fingers

existing solely

between optic nerve

and memory's delay

stimulate belief

in unknowable misconceptions

stand me between words

held with each finger's brief lingering

make me desire

no ancient papers

deliver me

from arcane quill shadows

find home

within imagined circumstances

letters existing without ink

syllables conducting

liberated dances on palms

replaced

colors' presence overshadows nightmarish brightness

subdue in me extremities' white compulsions

free necessity from sentiment

break tradition out of perfection's sought prison

modern fortress of lust not simply for flesh

utopia's absence waits unacknowledged

while riots mold new bricks to separate

dig irrigation trenches to drown truths

bridges burned before their consecration

champagne commemorations become flaming cocktails

gradiented viewpoints' popularity

fails to attract clemency before their summary

    executions

life no longer vibrates in varied frequencies

daily moments' shifts of opinion

stay in bed

expressions of carnal flexibility

brutally eschewed

replaced

classification trumps understanding

belonging superseding inclusion's once-pervading view
       of species siblings

rivalry's skirmishes now trench warfare

pressed faked realities' headlines draw maps of exclusion

changed climates regress to shadowed corners of
       rounded globes

self-interest

giving's replacement

hate

the love of tomorrow

snowflakes

misunderstood selves cringe before mirrors

where visions are clouded by judgment

imposed yet swallowed as supplement in lieu of

comprehension

too much time to learn

busy is necessity

videos streamed in endless feline progressions

dinner and drinks overshadow images of self-loathing

once on display

now stored in closets once reserved for sexual secrets

those on display before notifications of fuckfriends'

complexity

no question periods remain

once interrogation denounced amid guileless depictions

of inquisition's perpetual absence of stupidity

no longer spoken

as grammatical markers of reciprocal curve and point

fade from use

answers' necessity implied as left

without comment

wardrobe before substance once detailed public

existence

today's self-expression

artifice of self-denunciation

depictions of broken minds

detract interest's validity

yourself

expression not required

constructed being's personality

i am my profile

music's streams

lutes become ephemeral existences of frequencies

ears no longer strained by analog warping

fidelities reaching for heights impossible to reach

without chemical intervention

yet beauty remains often unsought

more still unrequited

tender auralities satisfied through penetrations'

minimalisms

to trust performances' authenticities

delight in timeless sonorous reproductive rites

yet worlds become subverted in their separateness

blocked from presents' existence through playback

spoken words in nows have no force to distract

thoughts of auditory nirvana

listeners dwelling on clouds of mite-inspired delusion

today ceases to be

we are saved from humans

by sounds' ubiquity

finally

unmarked questions

believe me

we are no longer

not dead

simply without the necessity

to exist

to breathe life into thought

as thought is become deceased

burial abhorred

the enemy of truth may be deceit

but faith's enemy

it is not infidelity, yet questions

answers irregardless

those around us live

without elucidation

interrogations left unbegun

unremarked undesired

sadly unnoticed

inquiries limit themselves to banalities

depth

an affront to freedom

doubt become faithful obsession

no longer a society of religion

the only sin is to ask

equality of positions' value

no longer questioned

simply extant

assumed as fundamental right

inhuman yet pervasive

the voice of many

shouts over few's whispers

to be right

scream

we listen only to the loud

even

pages unturned yet curiously incomprehensible

in post-enlightenment's dark age

cynicism become state religion

neopaganism's church infected by disinterest

worships distraction

passivity secedes from consciousness' desires

active lethargy stands in

bedclothes' appeal is their statement

i cannot even

be asked to

think

not once as the self is all there is

responsibility falls unused

tonight's assumed drunkenness

fulfills expectations of simulated poverty

self-selected disenchantment

no longer revolutionary

conscious objections from sobriety

mirrors' comprehensions

beyond acceptable levels of painful

rejected as unhelpful

a world of self-interest

become nothing more than whimsical

immediacy

impetus begets reaction

processing delayed as scandalous

be

react

do not think

desire

what is this desire of which you speak

drive for humans distant from my mind

excuse for models self-imposed of sin

guilt's dark secret brought to screens' light

you cry forgiveness' hopes yet act

in ways evil seeming cannot detach

no resistance appears in moments

justification by hormone falls flat on my ears

yet each moment no derision comes

but regret

you entertain others with games prescribed

inquiring to motives for repeated engagement

i lose myself in inquisition's mask

while you are led by lust's

shattered self-image

depths

cannot you speak

of those things unseen

that travel within minds' darkest corridors

and place themselves

not into the light

of understandings' gazes of many

where knowledge within you

shifts from importance

to inconsequential lust

for impressions made and lost

in moments

but replaced with a comprehension

taking no notes

yet seeking fundamentals' friction

and tacit tensions

within facts' antecedents

between hairs' color and lips' lives

breathes sleeps wakes

another possible stand

wherein you meet an earth

recreated as images torn

from pages unwritten

yet imagined

mind screams forth in silence

begging nothing but perceptions' alternatives

to obviousness' failure

to engender life

within belief

beauty exists

beyond concrete realities' feeble grasp

of presents tenuous

and fleeting

look past rote truths' limiting sadnesses

to possibilities' freedoms' learnings

remember not

think simply

breathe minds' life

to deep places yet unexplored

skin

here's illusionary presence dispels notions

of your presence beside me

you from away cannot possibly equal me

they say

liberal dictations flowing to the contrary from lips

       plentiful

attached to bodies inactive

they tell me equality sells

inherent humanity become political tool

i believe yet i have been discredited

they speak

you are from elsewhere

not like us

difference praised in words

foundation for hatreds myriad

wars unceasing

rape

unending introspection targeted

i am not of here

they see me as sister

you know

i am closer to you

but we seek not to overthrow

overwhelm

solely overcome to share hilltops

while valleys flood from damns

lips speaking them in silence

they force their words through my lips

identities' fears of loss

tomorrow their eyes may focus on my otherness

now is grief at my implied position

artifice is pale skin covering minds of varied colors

one

speak in my ear while i do my best not to listen

to what you have to say

savoring the taste of your voice in my mind

language irregardless

text unnecessary

speak only to the sensations that tongue transmits

touch not skin but shape new images within me

images of fragmentary desire

momentary ideals

beauty in your reflection with each charged breath's
        brush

not of hair but memory

be not yourself alone

combine with me not through insertion

through speaking

while cohesions' melded joins form

one in swallowed intent

two unnecessary in conjoined expression

when truly i desire you in mind

humanities' importances cease their dominance

souls' energies' transformations' collected to new views

tremors from underground tracts

cisterns given way to aqueducts long dry

flowing from streams of connected comprehension

self fallen away

summarily redrawn from principles of other

become me

touch my soul with your tongue from afar
listen not to words
breathe thoughts direct within my mind
translate your memories for me that i desire you
not for play but
lexical gymnastics

be within me
become me

breathe me so i see through your
eyes

taste with your
fingers

smile through your

lips

stained

glass' self-separations cast shadows' fragmentary hues

marble's white resembling dye become untied

coherence dispersed teaches

the whole need not be less than parts' sums

while expectations dictate myself as pasts' unquestioning

offspring

no more than mild divergence from nation's self-image

become manifest

the individual alive and well in death

your reflection i am and you me

expression replacing action

itself become token wildness

farther from last night's accepted with each passed

generation

flamboyance replacing substance

if ever such was

liberal posts stand where racist diatribes once held sway

covering hatreds no longer spoken

more engrained as days pass

hidden as once loves' bent expressions cowered in

        cultures' closets

eros' passions overwhelm sisters' hopes

ecstasies' claim of all moments engages new dialectics

of stages of us

we embrace as lovers or i am them

other

significant in your speech somehow desired no more

        than as unpredictable stimulus

my thoughts if not yours

invalid

try?

know through breaths' depths yourself

tomorrows' endless stretches write unrhymed futures

unbounded

why in mirrors' faces speak silver-lined voices tarnished

before failures' potentials instantiate as real

no loss so deep occurs than that of forfeited attempts

but perhaps trials' unmotivated beginnings

departed to time unending before they are born

think not possibilities

positives help nothing when negatives engender panic

harmony arrives not on roads paved with inaction

or conflict

simply through accepted counterpoint

with each moment

placing chords of sound beauty in paths once shadowed

dissonance of self-loathing

intertwined with reflections' skewed stained glass

       mirrors

speak to your own mind in questions

others' as equal

we act from thought and pause in expectation

to think through movement is

feathered lightness of spirit

playing bridge

wavetops cast ephemeral shadows beyond existences'
     sightlines
beautiful only in their negative space
relentlessnesses pummel imaginary breakwaters
penetrating defenses' limits to seek sanctuary for violent
     images
within where remains a haven when boundaries fall not
     as dominos
but papers' rice folds of undesired messages' flimsies
safety presents solely in numbers' overwhelming force
selves' sanctities cast as pink-reflected freshwater spheres
consumed by mass hysterias' frenzied followings
there is now choice
remain to be disintegrated

forgotten as never having existed

turn walk flee become backs' visions of victimhood

escape simply a morphed reincarnation of bruising

nine-tailed words spill existentially inconsequent red

       liquids

rumors' chattering gently inserts itself beneath nude

       armor

speak consent's critique of common capitulation

to rooms of rights' self-declared champions

who hear silences' virginities echo where syllables

       bounce back

finding their tonguelashed origins before ears open

dissimulation carries covering scents

one sees woman standing not scorned but ignored

majorities' insignificance in one being

truth changes nothing in its reverberation

diatribes of worthlessness conceal understanding gazes

todays' foundations would crumble if she were heard

believed

yet you dismissed her

they are safe

mornings after

you stand as a shrine

enlightened shadow of seshat's scriptural tenets

incarnate within my memories' imaginings

somehow though commensurate with ballpoint touches

      on fresh leaves

why that image when paper dissolves in antiquities'

      grasps

replaced by summarily present contacts multiplied

      tenfold

digital plastic communion sanctified by pixel-perfect

      prosody

whining echoes of bloodstained traumas

lost to all but the broken through disinformation's fires

none but ash left of you whose first flame

was extinguished by experience

you lie as speaker

resonating darkness from souls' depths

onto guided targets' forgotten senses

become self again

walk in imagined forests

where shimmering distant tree peaks

carve lazy arcs through astral clouds

bend your story to words

say your truth against ears

wrapped in shrouds

mornings' death of your freedom

comes

with last nights' plentiful gendered acts

receiving spirits' overflowing energies

unauthorized

dams' shattered stones reflected in your verses

to spoken tongues trapped by disbelief

taste bitter pasts to unbound eyes

you need not convince any longer

say

to me

from heights of babel lofty and unexplored i fell
grace caught not a feather of my weight
impact delayed only by disbelief
thought transcending unreality
at the idea i could have lived untruths in your eyes

ears mine and others swam in dark waters
collapsing at your feet in profuse supplication
you averted senses not only visual
words and notes no longer possible
unhearing became your new default stance

they know me not yet doubts' benefits were possible
while your back was my mind's only view

i could ask for no other cheek to be turned

the first one having been unoffered

no forgiveness is necessary

only faith

loss

collide with my soul

dearest beauty transcendent

your life's lyrics dance coital precursors

with joy uncompromising

behind your eyes

yet somehow within my memory

tricks played therein

but you and only you consume me

as i believe fulfills today's deepest hope

leave not for a moment

my conscious presence

even in distances' necessities of each day apart

you live as oil overwhelming sailcloth

beneath optic stimulation

preaching gospels of protest you lie

new muse to decades of digital content

reaching out to touch pixels

somehow undesirous yet forthcoming

cause me to speak of your mind

transformed through languages' rich tapestries

woven between experiences' myriad fantasies

as you talk through my ears

lyrics from my lips at one step

removed from pictures i created without artistry

polished in your image to portray

revolution's banners of days' newnesses

spread on streets paved silver in their unlined reflections

spiritual cohesion converts my tears

love swims through fonts immortal and self-fulfilling

in your absence you live in me

ripples

we live as if there is no afterlife

yet we forget we need no scripture

to teach us of our parents

grandparents burned into our existence

genetics unnecessary for memory's progression

family stories abound yet

there is no nature

we do nothing through a priori ideas

as thought has no language

but what we learn today

yesterday echoes endlessly

to futures' unseen terminals

we may wish to silence ourselves

go so far as to attempt

even succeed

death has no hold over us

only bodies

wrapped parcels of energy

unstrung from brown papers' tenuous grips

children become our aftereffects

not simply ours

we are many

speaking among not alone

this present

tomorrows' tessellated foundations

we shall not end

tradition is our resurrection

even in rejection

reaction is memory

fear not death's illusionary

ends

forgive

direct confluence of thoughts

between emotion and actions' absence

lies untruthfully

within the confines of broken

dreams' guilty indulgences

of fancies airborne and unyielding

resurrect me

from sensations cross

and indulgently complex

to stand fluidly

while vicious waters convert assumptions

of gentle caresses to groping fingers

seeking nothing short

of spirits' disintegration

turn memories' fuzzy illogic
to tool of futures' calmnesses
no longer to be assaulted
and sent beneath earths' fields
of mourning in assemblies of disinformation
become pasts' signposts

breathe lives' brutal immediacies
through moments' uncertainties
to pleasure sensations' doubts
and enliven unseeing selves
trapped by regrets'
unending circles of sorrow

walk through shadows' hilltop intercessions

to drink quietnesses' instantaneous self-forgiveness

with celebrations' belief

not in tomorrows' possibilities

but this now's art of being

sensations

i breathe

as if there is no moment

but the one in which i find

myself indulging in sensations deep

and simultaneously unsubtle

that take me from a feeling of apprehension

to that of pure and unadulterated panic

both immediate and ephemerally everlasting

an image of faith

not simply lost but alive and well

in its questioning fluidity

gives me imaginary ideas of comfort

but grounds me to an earth

beyond unstable

yet somehow collapsing

under the weight of realities' unnecessary influence

ubiquitous terrorism of the soul

denies me escape

as i may avail myself

of flights' fancy opportunities

in the face of disasters external and human

but within i am interred

while gasping breaths' undesired life

and fanciful dreams distract not a moment

fear's consumptions become clockwork

before eyes unmoving

in adrenaline's paralysis

not of motion alone

but thought adhered to potentialities' improbabilities

made certainties to spite pleasures' impossibilities

no longer hoped for if unseen

awakenesses project auras of impermanence

during ages of compassionless eternity

unyielding in its solemnity

ritually contrasting minds' inherent charged skirmishes

with indecision's secluded admissions

of efforts' unforeseen absenteeism

welcome

truths' unnecessary adjuncts

to memories' pasts' imaginings

shade shameful decisions

not simply untaken

yet permanent

in your imaginations' wakeful dreams

you sleep more peacefully

with nightmares founded

on happenings forgotten

and restless

than days' open-eyed despairings

deeply seated

in beliefs' creations

you stand in self-judgement

when lies' surrounding armies

penetrate flesh

with swords' points

of humans' desperate lust

for ephemeral melodies' indulgent lyrics

of interpreted irrationality

you are laid out of state

on faults shimmering

in quakes unfelt

beyond your skin

yet triggered through ideas' sensations

from the mouths of enemies undeclared

of uncertainties' wars

you became trapped

yet somehow breathe

phoenixes of disillusionment

long awaited yet unanticipated

in the face of ideals

beyond absences of concern

hate lives in the many

while you scream silent curses

against its implied victory

your freedom shimmers

through hazes of protest

without idolatry's speech

action in itself

is your weapon of self-defense

time is become your ally

in its impermanence

creation

lies are beauties' truths

spoken in ears primed by misunderstanding

perception of worlds' sights

impervious to your ministrations of belief

yet somehow shaped by interpretation

branches' leaves formed

in line with photographs' transformations

iterative beauty in absence of language

depicts absence

no thought appears

without text absence obliterates all

more than spoken words' echoes

no earth is possible

rain falls only in your understanding

forests silent without ears

darkness overwhelms in lights' absences

intimacies' touches grow cold

in sleep's asensual depths

talk life to spirits' echoes

i live only in your tongue

speaking verse to depict

what cameras' presences no more than obscure

once

spheric sonorities shimmer

echoing between stone faces' tacit existences

giving nothing of themselves

yet shaping ears' interpretations

by the simplicity

of their curved natures

within your eyes

feel gradual attenuation of movement

toward geological inaction

but sleep not on your feet

as you drink earth's dancing plainsong

interrupted by jays' calls

beyond horizons once eliciting

ideas of limitlessness

you have again been called

from dream to places not awake

yet somehow behind

contemporary realities' hold

on present stereotyping

of the moment

penetrate veiled memories' defenses

to swim naked

in shuttered forests' streams

atop viciously cloud-harnessed mountains

suddenly relieving doubtful reminiscences

toward beauties' future necessities

breathe sunstroked elicitations of petals

gradiented from shadows' purple

to pinks' radiant translucences

as mirrors not visual

yet spiritual in their untimid requests

for personal awakenings

lie within unviewed trenches

of minds' subtle creation

from past imaginings' minglings

in lands unadulterated

by objectivities' painful unrealities

so to rest unsleeping and absorb

new worlds of desire

unfulfilled recollections of love

burrow to new depths

within once-grieving contemplations

yet uncover purities unexpected

beneath maturities' gazes

shoulder glances

within dreams' unyielding presence

lie untruths awaiting acceptance

as reformed and rewritten paradigms

of histories' reinterpreted desires

to replace past happinesses

with newly minted despair

unfulfilled hopes mingle

whisked toward rigid peaks

of loneliness once unfelt

yet remembered

with no sense of their inherent artifice

created in the image of hopelessness

to reflect days' experiences

no longer bright

in shadows' contemplative echoing depths

transforming laughter to tensions' breaths

heavy within chests

banded by rendered belts

of perceptions' creation

if the once encountered self

lives only in minds' eyes

peering over shoulders

with focus unwavering

in its intensity

for iterated duplications

of present pains

it may be a curse

to approach dawns

as anything

not slated

blanks

of tomorrows improvisational

behaviors' unprecedented

flit between cavern limitations

rising ever nearer

with each ideated untruth

breathing life

toward trending patterns

once ephemeral

become fixed endlessnesses

unbreakable in severities' consequence

of fates' retribution

clarion

eyes open

to the blackened remains

of cultures' ash

devolved and blinkered

by biases' revisionist fantasies

shed futures prescriptions

for apocalyptic uncoverings

of unprescient self-fulfillments

solely on the bases

of popularity contests'

manufactured beauty

disbelief

is no longer prescribed

as supplementary therapy

for the young

seeking skies

of gradiented greys

and mingled seatones

not yet elective self-medication

somehow degenerated

to ubiquitous illegality

where faith returns

to blindness

obligations amass

as dunes' unwalking shadows

creep ever closer

to following fictitious lemmings' footsteps

in seeming vertical self-abnegation

while shoulder angels scream obviousness

from sidelines

sheltered from vision

by chocolate-flavored acceptance

intoxicated staggering

becomes baseline normalcy

when doomsday scenarios

turn to separation fences' construction

and concrete monstrosities segregate

behind protectionist pasts' ignorings

of their inclusionary origin myths

turning all indentured subservients

to corporations' ethical edits

unfaithful

scriptures' daily rewritings

call out to us

across history's construction

of pending realities

unrealized

yet somehow communicated

as desired

in spite of their apparent silliness

great teachers' words

skew support in translation

for two-sided arguments

in demonstrations of ephemeral armies

facing themselves

in glass-floored iterative refractions

out of context

spoken words

in cathedrals of manipulated minds

decimate arches' grandeur

to trample mortal necessities

newly crushed

beneath their crumbled stones

never to be extracted

loves die

in gamified regrets

and procedural adherences

where she speaks words of code

to which he attributes

uncontextualized historical narrative

and his actions

become training

for his replacements' interpretative degeneration

epistolary messages

create instantaneous guidance

across millennia

where snowflakes' darkened frost

implies faithful worship

of false concepts' infallibilities

and the resurrection of thoughts

best left in stone-capped tombs

todays

lyric self-image stands in critical opposition

to realities' reflected perceptions

themselves unknowingly glassy-eyed

high on historical narratives

of people of similar hue

living in centuries more distant

than those of today

trapped behind walls of failed tomorrows' promises

built in the image of todays' misunderstood generations

unyielding in scope

yet admission of misogynist guilt

and racist untruths

told not full-voice

but in falsettos' shaded disbeliefs

to myriad children of unfaithful self-interest

knowing only screenshotted approximations

of identity

uncreated within the mind

unexpressed behind eyes

unmoved from hands' perspectives

impossible to differentiate from dance

performed on permanent stages

trampled to flatlined submission

where recovery is accepted as

impossible

yet not even hoped for

as our millennial dreams

reach only downward

gazes fixed on survival

expression of no more than

displeasures' weak echoes

unheard outside our ears

protest

nothing is lost

on those who have

misplaced their desire to hear

as listening becomes

forgotten art

and write-only pasts

determine future hopes

beliefs' formations

from shadowed bases

of dead forest shrubs

climb disintegrating ivy

toward skies

of carbons' undated armageddons

today is iteratively subverted

through endless retakes' divergence

only one footstep

from the mean

yet enough to appear distant

revolution resurrected

yet no more than slightly

while protections' lefts

battle harsh hatreds' allies

over word choice

in declarations of unindependence

days disappear

faced with exploration of meaning

distantly undesired

while spoken of

with respectful tones

reminiscent of the animation

of generations past

absence of all

beyond formal inheritances of verisimilitudes

that disappear

the moment they are taken

from their screen-bound selves

kaddish unspoken

in dry rooms

oppressive in their secret exclusion

for ideas once screamed

from very walls

of marching protest

silent

in the face of triumph

defeated

by preemptive dissolution of interest

inside voices

cardboard and magic markers
scream silenced slogans
beneath overhanging deprecations'
harsh consonants

preaching
to unsung antiheroes' ears

change is fear
made incarnate in eyes
trapped within bodies
of hatred
fleeing before onrushing
foreign thoughts

challenging

an ethic of lust

swallow depths

of unbreathable lacrymal stimulants

surrounded by compatriots

without unreflective homelands' biases

not thinking

is today's only existence

who listens not

to mass hysteria

but oppressed voices

singing through ash-blackened veils

on street corners

assumed to be members
of ancient professions
whose only penetrations
are unspoken protests
of violations long past
yet unforgettable

speech
no longer makes you free

stones

concentric arcs disappear toward shimmering calms

each breaking stride against its neighbors' fences'

      encroachments

heaven's increasing drops mesh toward lake's ideal

      mirror

single images quickly become fragments

hope for cohesion dispelled

intersected circles' self-integration gives shadow to

      clouds' failed attempts at lights' rebellion

      through hovering liquid

where once i glimpsed myself

now stand myriad mes

deformed to points unexpected echoing to horizons'
      hopeful ends
i conceived no self-brokenness on such scales

as thoughts once clear reflect as multiplied divergences
no possibility to stand together remains
would it were possible to assemble not as humans but
      one

yet divisive rhetoric instantiates segregated sisters

chances to walk miles in other shoes
imply representative non-selves
an idea of times past
eras when place
and past

experience stood behind tradition

i am told

identity obviates beauty's necessity

majorities' beliefs overshadow unpopular views

equality

speak words of reflexive aggrandizement into shadowy

      repeating chambers

glass houses beg stones' fracturing flights
i shan't be the first among equals

do not

it may be possible to seek to find
doubtful though
happiness is not a myth
but it soars on passive wings

accept not the hate neighbors' rivers flow with
believe freely
give thoughts reins' lack of blinkers
yet joy grows from silence

not minds' disengagement
simply silks' frictionless mental planes
coursing through veins of wonder
be still

and know you are

even unspoken

ideal

coherence devolves ungovernable

behind doors eternally unopened

forever trapped within snowfalls

heavy with merits' unrecognized

truths shattered by shadows' inhabitants

wielding unfocused batons

of disinformation

and whips of untamed hatred

cracked against prebroken backs

fragmented as inherent ideals

shimmer in disappearance

on streets' unaligned

ends

undead yet lifeless

concentric squares of homeless sensations

squirm in unripened grains'

fields of interference

patterns

sensed but ambiguously unimportant

lost amid flowers of a single petal

reaching toward proximate stars' warmth

eclipsed not by losna's reflection

but disbelief's shield of translucent innocence

where descends light

when diffracting screams

act crystal to peaces' whimpers

not unheard

purely abandoned

afterlives

mere moments of knees

brushing woven grass imitations

of amaterasu's forest floors

devolve perceptions' dominances

to forgotten traumas

of lives no longer present

in unlivable memories

resurrected across

times' unfixed loops

circles unbroken

but for deaths' insignificant vantages

on pasts immemorable

in undeciphered stanzas

written in transparent inks

on echoes' waves

between winds' sighing

unpredictability enfold futures

dreamed for

without design

tomorrows' yesterdays dance

as leaves' partners

to fūjin's unbroken

lyric intercessions

amid unspeakable enervations

behind eyes' trembling nerves

while stone walls' unyielding projections

inhabit trainees' gazes

giving to skies' unclouded judgments

momentary identities

reverberations' breathed melodic drives

subvert movement desires

with cyclic streams

no longer purely digital visions

for uncovered ears

while petals dispel

gravities' harsh unambiguity

and turn to the proximity

of bamboo's

silken coverings

opened eyes' unseeing light

drinks absent visions

from igneous histories' tales

of fiery rebirth

beyond shivering lands

whispered flutes

imagined between mountain faces

tremble over rippled visions

of dragonflies' wings

the fall

clouded visions catch thermals
altitudes increasing
while distances between us
shrink

yet somehow differences
become further entrenched
approaching spheric centers
with each shovel's twitch

minor youths sing poignant chords
distressed beyond denim's limits
tears flowing through damned lips
parched as from diminishing fluidity

only walking frees us from truths' unholy embrace

torture without concrete necessity

chains futures to notes passed

behind secret transparent ceilings

we voice calls to overcome

but violent rebellion

attracts none

who are not yet sinking

and whose drowned lyrics are written

on pages' unyielding disappearances

become blackened smoke before ink smears their

       integrity

collapsed onto winds unchanging

About the Author

Avi is a teacher and writer, one who desires to live outside the boundaries of a society lost to the artifice of equality trampled by misogyny, racism, and sexualized oppression, one who lives apart from the constructions of gender identity while crying for the necessity of that existence being apart from a world in fragments because of its unwillingness to shed its traditional attachment to manufactured roles.

They have lived and studied between Canada's east and west coasts, composing poetry on the shores of the Atlantic and pacific, holding dear within the heart the solitude that comes from standing at the edge of land with feet no longer willing to turn back toward humanity's lost humanity.

They are a proponent of art as an unrelenting walk along the pathway of beauty where ideas and thoughts and reality and existence take secondary role to language as a conduit for the simple pleasure of words living for their capacity to take the listener, the reader, even the writer to new worlds deep not in their knowledge but in their pure escape into beauty itself.

> *in thought truth may arrive*
>
> *or perhaps it remains absent*
>
> *yet without a desire to know*
>
> *lies shall be your only sanctuary*

It's in these divisions that the various interpretations of the bicameral systems of government began to emerge, bringing with it all these associations bound up with the functions of public life we in the States identify as the House of Representatives, with its upper and lower chambers. Thus encoded, our systems of government, with their expectation of a system of self-representation, seems to hobble along, albeit at times along a much more clear, if continuously imperfect seeming path. My approach has been to question those directly affected by this invisibility or exclusion of personhood in the art-cultural and larger socio-cultural orders of the polis as field research into these essentialist notions and, it's worth noting, from specific perspectives that I think of as tracing an arc where art and ideology often align, around notions of identity-formation often associated with our notions of the body. Still, even and especially shrouded in the machinery of modernity, how that self should best be defined often fails to adhere across cultures, subject to the machinations of petty despots. Our laws, emanating from our national self-rule, in their aspiration to a state of nature, span history polluted with petty personal and shared, spiteful grievances, most often expressed by pointing out the differences between human beings, as if evidence of one or another people's natural superiority to those they're comparing themselves.

It's a line of inquiry, as it turns out, with a rich historicity. Charles Taylor, who I will often cite, and almost entirely find agreement with on pretty much everything he's written, talks a lot about the historical role of artists within the coalescing standards of courtly life, where learned civility displaced the aristocracy as the ultimate measure of status, and as the force of a universally-mobilized collective kind of self-preservation. Civility clearly serves to cyclically replace the ritual bloodshed of the honor-ethic as a recipe, for instance, to rebuke the ghastly violence of the Crusades as a collective standard for the demands placed upon human survival by acting within the undeniable dictates of natural law. Driven by the honor-ethic, cycles of violence dictated stature for centuries. Impossible standards are suicidal; not unique in any way, today retributive violence doesn't function as a global system for binding human interest except in large parts of the social imaginary. Still, if social imaginaries are, as John Thompson wrote, "the creative and symbolic dimension of the social world, the dimension through which human beings create their ways of living together and their ways of representing their collective life,"[3] then aren't artists somehow central to the construction of that dimension?

Yes, and there exist orgiastic amounts of evidence. Still, I'd always wished there was more discovery done as to the truth of that proposition, especially as concerns the identity-formation process of artists in any socially-prescribed state of exclusion, people without moral country or welcome port, forced to survive despite established norms; instead, there's a lack of analysis outside a pronounced fascination with celebrity *other-worldliness* as regards how artists see *themselves*. This is, notably, also a symptom of Western civilization's maladaptation to the voices and presence of whole spectrums of people outside patriarchal, classist, white supremacist foundational models of artistic representation. And something I've, with a great deal of intentionality, sought to direct my own work against, as I hope is clear from this collection. I'm especially proud of the number of Movement Matters columns included, as they will be throughout the series. These columns, focusing on dance and its instrumentalization of the body as art-making material, slow evolution, emergence into the avant garde, and current transformations, are meant as one critique among many, but one of special focus within the project, of the mainstream limitation of current art critical subjects of reference.

3 John B. Thompson, *Studies in the Theory of Ideology*, University of California Press, 1984, p. 6

It's also worth noting that the entire Movement Matters series serves as field research for a collection of choreographed social interactions, performance scores and instructions I've been writing over the years. "Intimate Conversation," the first performance from this body of work to be presented in public, was also the first published score, included in *Propositional Attitudes*, a collection edited by Elana Mann and John Burtle, and released through Golden Spike Press.

Directly related to this new, emerging strain I've taken to describing as "instructional art," Movement Matters has served as a jumping-off point for other score-writing that extends the range of focus, such as the *Night Moves* series, organized around interactions in places where people gather in the evening hours. Otherwise, each score serves as the elaboration of concerns brought up in the interviews, or through symposia organized each season that are, separately, in development as an artist-produced documentary series investigating the intersections of interaction, politics, policy, dance, performance, social practice art, and notions "in the air."

In art-historical context, we find further jurisprudential sources to the political tension of these concerns in the work of some of our most compelling artists. We find in Goya, for example, an understanding how violent horrors, often and especially state-sponsored or "from above," were insuperable from the experience of religious persecution. This strain in its socially-engaged aspects emerge post-1900 into a paramount proposition that art *should* shift realities, and bring the public into alignment with an imagined ideal to improve the social bond. Here, too then, we see an echo of and a need for improvement of the rules that govern "interactions between people." If artists do demonstrate what Taylor would describe as even a "half-way house" of self-awareness in processing what effects of modernization they had experienced, how compelling the question, then, in what manner they would aspire to effect their own life-direction. Of course, I can't leave out what Wayne Booth would describe as the "implied author" aspect of this inquiry. For me, it has been further compelling to see if there were commonalities in the values defined among my various subjects, and how they were or were not reflected in the evolution of my own values, outlooks and approaches to art-making. In that sense, this project has long bobbed along at a selfishly observational cruising speed for me and was, in some sense, a way of opening an investigation into where the notion of voluntary self-formation occurred to me in my own experience.

In the course of this investigation, there are innumerable things I've come to admire about the people I've spoken with over the years. There's a sense in which self-conception is already formed against, and often in diametric opposition to the problems of the world's central institutions, the stakes of this identification, the shortcomings, strivings, cherished successes and of an incessant need to pursue the improvement of both self and what confrontations or resistances Husserlian *lebenswelt*, or "lifeworld" may demand. I've sought what may be described as moments where the meeting points of public opinion and art culture have resulted, through the conversion of shared experience, into an affirmation of some new cultural good. Again, an explicit goal of the historical avant-garde, to "repair the social bond," in societies atomized by the dictates of instrumental reason, dehumanized by neoliberalism, with its inevitable militarization, capital, technology and the ascent of scientistic reductivisms, and a generalized disillusionment by the move away from hierarchies of nature, has often resulted in the express desire to restore some baseline of human perspective.

Aspirational as that outcome may often be, I began to wonder how other artists think their work contributes to the definition and expansion of what's referred to in philosophic circles as the "social imaginary."

That is,

" ... something much broader and deeper than the intellectual schemes people may entertain when they think about social reality in a disengaged mode. I am thinking, rather, of the ways people imagine their social existence, how they fit together with others, how things go on between them and their fellows, the expectations that are normally met, and the deeper *normative notions and images*[4] that underlie these expectations.

There are important differences between social imaginary and social theory. I adopt the term imaginary (i) because my mind is on the way ordinary people "imagine" their social surroundings, and this is often not expressed in theoretical terms, but is carried in images, stories, and legends. It is also the case that (ii) theory is often the possession of a small minority, whereas what is interesting in the social imaginary is that it is shared by large groups of people, if not the whole society. Which leads to a third difference: (iii) the social imaginary is that common understanding that makes possible common practices and a widely shared sense of legitimacy."[5]

Taylor's endlessly brilliant, and correct to ground his definitions of the "common practices" against this background in *oikonomos*, the outgrowths of which serve as a root source of neoliberal ideals. I am also further compelled by his corollary citation of Grotius as a starting-point in *Modern Social Imaginaries*, as "a theory of what a political society is, that is, what it is in aid of, and how it comes to be. But any theory of this kind also offers inescapably an ideal of moral order: it tells us something about how we ought to live together

---

4   Emphasis mine.
5   Taylor, Charles, *Modern Social Imaginaries*, Duke University Press, 2004, p. 23.

in society."[6] As the first to propose a notion of an international community, and of its grounds in a range of conflicting interests, Grotius' concerns obviously share widely compelling stakes, especially at points in history where our axial foundations have begun to fray the seams of social fabric in ways that threaten a destabilization of the whole, as between cosmopolitanism and nationalism in the grip of resurgent fascism, for instance. We know from thinkers such as Zigmunt Bauman, expounding on Hannah Arendt and others, that the two are not mutually exclusive in the processes of modernity's imposition of "stranger" statuses on certain groups, often including artists and those not so easily organized into prescribed societal roles. This notion of exclusion elides well, for instance, with imposed "states of exception" as Giorgio Agamben has delineated extensively, and particularly his analysis of the *aucturitas*, with its claims of governmental legitimacy intrinsically tied to the physical embodiment of a ruling authority, dictator or other kind of autocrat. It's a power that contemporary Jacques Ranciere asserts Agamben views as a "state of exception with the power of decision over life,"[7] echoing Habermas above, and that Agamben defines in its most extreme examples as "the establishment, by means of the state of exception, of a legal civil war that allows for the physical elimination not only of political adversaries but of entire categories of citizens who for some reason cannot be integrated into the political system."[8]

It's helpful to have the recent historic precedents of their work to frame-in these notions, by example, in this common goal of defining what Foucault would famously characterize as proofs *dispositif.* Rather than getting bogged down into comparison of

---

6   Ibid, , p. 3.
7   Ranciere, Jacques , "Who is the Subject of the Rights of Man?" *South Atlantic Quarterly*, 2004, 103(2–3):297–310.
8   Agamben, Giorgio, *States of Exception*, University of Chicago Press, 2005, p. 2.

endlessly opposed political currencies, it's my intention here to echo the Taylorian principle of centering on Platonic Forms, with much of the parameters of modern imaginaries rooted early-on in staving off widespread religious conflict and rebellion against the ruling authorities. Along these lines, it's familiar how much art has strove to tread intermediary roles across the post-axial changes he identifies. In terms of the interview subjects selected for this volume, I've strove to pluck out the roles of modern differentiation in these forms against the backgrounds I've been discussing, not just of any particular visual or art cultural history, but in its most expansive possible sense: what art forms we may discuss in this context *as a social whole*. I've sought to know who artists *think* they are, and to follow those bread crumbs where they may lead, in hopes of giving a more equal voice artistically, whether ensconced in canon, barely visible, or rendered entirely invisible, in the dominant moment. To that end, I've also included a few others, such as activists recognized for their agitation after greater equality, whose creative action is bent to the manifestation of an improved world.

In each case, I've tried to talk as little as possible, and listen. In another sense, they represent the start to a culmination of half my lifetime's inquiry into how art is thought, its ideas disseminated, resisted, elevated, transformed into weapons, transformed across social norms and values; these and a seemingly infinite list of potential variables are at the heart of the question how we should best conduct our "living together," though, for many, it signals a cosmopolitan tolerance and acceptance of, at best, "foreign" perspectives, worthy of violent response. American life is benighted with multiple daily reminders of the way casual acceptance of violence against those exceptions to the norms of our way of life is stitched into our social fabric, such that we've long since become inured to its presence. This represents an instrumentalization that extends back through industrialization, a disenchantment with modern life that inevitably occurs, and that reflects the point of neoliberal pograms of cultural interpolation into democratic, pluralistic sources of state power that rival the atrocities of Mao's cultural purges.

In fact, white power movements, patriarchy and the straining demands of unrestricted capital continue to drive aspects of most past governmental structures to play out this selfsame dynamic, with its familiar refrains of insular, exclusionist power domination, to the point that its influence as an ideal seems repulsive to our post-Enlightenment ears. Yet, these schisms are allowed, and often encouraged in their persistence. Having been raised during the culture wars of the early '80's and '90's in the States, it's yet remarkable how much, for instance, the background understanding of poverty as a sacral state of existence, and of the ways in which society made room for or refuted those wrenched into precarity, began to percolate into social-informational schisms, and were used to justify the subtle consolidation of bigotries that seem tame next to today's endless reduction of sex, gender and race differences to "incivility," or "obscenity," which has now come to mirror our own recent outright enshrinements of hatred into the life cycles of much legislative and juridical stone.

There exist orgies of abandoned junk jurisprudence and legal precedent that testifies to the ability of these white power movements to pervert of our various government branches, often rooted in erecting barriers to miscegenation, as poignantly described in James Q. Whitman's extraordinary work on the taxonomies in American race law that led directly to the legalization of radically efficient, industrialized murder-solutions to race differences under Nazism.

> It is a familiar fact that much of America was infected with
> the same race madness: as the Nazi literature noted, there were
> plenty of Americans who simply "knew" that black men regularly

raped white women. American courts, as German authors were aware, were capable of delivering matter-of-fact holdings such as "the mixing of the two races would create a mongrel population and a degraded civilization;" the American Supreme Court entertained briefs from southern states whose arguments were indistinguishable from those of the Nazis, and southern racists like Senator Theodore Bilbo, staunch supporter of the New Deal in the 1930s, could the tell of decay through the races every bit as wild-eyed as Helmut Nicolai's: "Pleading against 'mongrelization' in the anti-lynching debate of 1938, a process he claimed had destroyed white civilization over much of the globe, Bilbo took a page from Hitler's *Mein Kampf* to assert that merely 'one drop of Negro blood placed in the veins of the purest Caucasian destroys the inventive genius of his mind and palsies his creative faculty.'"[9]

Note that word, *creativity*. We'll come back to it below. Here, our "drop of blood" laws of racial impurity, for example, were thought too high a bar for the racial ravings of Nazism's newly-drafted legal standards. It makes sense, given this how, barred from specific roles within social life, choice came to assume a defining role in the selection of personhood, a way of excluding those "othered" from functions in society without the right to legal selfhood as defined by the state. You need only choose, and your choices will make you unique, goes the messaging, with all its echoes of Lockean political expediency. All of it, focused through the lens of righteous violence as the central power in humanity's fight for survival against, at times, the programmed interest in preservation of property and profit. Artists, all-too often a target of these enshrinements of hatred into state power, become targets, in attempts to control access through their work to education that might alter versions of program-approved social imaginary.

9 Whitman, James Q, *Hitler's American Model: The United States and the Making of Nazi Race Law*, Princeton University Press, 2017, p. 77.

Much of the United States' current experience of life under authoritarian rule demonstrates this, and reflects shifts in public messaging that combine mass media with frequent truth-blackouts to restrict information, simultaneously talking in despotic dogwhistles.

There's no shortage of foundational corollaries, of course, whether in the ghastly repugnancies of slavery or the genocides of the Westward Expansion, Japanese and recent Muslim internments, it's a list that stretches the length of human existence, one rooted in the central avant-garde recognition of a dehumanization that threatens the species, and a picking-apart of its processes. One may be forgiven asking, how and wherefore in this desperate political morass, then, art? Art-canon historically along these lines, as we've been discussing, this has meant an avant-garde in constant agitation for increasing the value of human life against the grandiose Molochs allowed to fester across institutional systems, whether evidenced by the irrepressible gun culture of the U.S. or the gleeful profiteering of our pharmaceutical industries that have led to a horrific, constantly outward-rippling opioid epidemic death toll. Neoliberal economic philosophies, applied to naked social engineering outcomes, have driven the bloodthirsty social projects of Pinochet and Reagan, Duterte and Trump. It's an old ideal. Rooted in the cultural psyche of the taming of the American West, the cowboy is a uniquely American colonial self-image that openly celebrates the genocidal extermination of indigenous peoples, for profit and out of sport for American urges to race hating ur-nation self-image of the *Pax Americana*. Emulated across mass culture, and a source of survivalist fear-cult obsessions, it's what let Senator Breckinridge espouse the notion that "a bad negro is the most horrible creature upon the earth, the most brutal and merciless," with all its capitalist assumption toward assembling arsenals and vast stores of resources to protect against such savages[10] and their threats of foreign invasion, with the supremacist tendencies that inform it epitomizing why an avant-garde was ever historically necessary. It was an alignment in repugnance to, and in mortal opposition against, any and all claims of moral superiority through violence.

Much avant-garde art of the 1960's and '70's explicitly thus sought to counter the narrative of the necessity of state-sponsored violence, a move that parallels the objective to dematerialize the art object throughout the same period. Perhaps a reaction to initial strains of neoliberalism "in the air," a fragmentation in how to approach the social relevance of art-making began to take place. It was during this period that John Cage and his Black Mountain compatriots presented what music critic Mark Swed writes was "widely credited as having been the first Happening and the inciter of performance art. Retrospectively it has been given the title '*Theater Piece No. 1*.'"[11] From this precedent, it seems clear members of the Judson Church scene devised the first shifts in virtuosity to result in avant-garde dance, a shift from which movement would later emerge as an art unto itself; and from this shift, a new choreographic dimension that mirrors the modernist self-markers of much new, body-derived habituations, and that also served to shift the planal concept of art's post-Abex dimensionality yet again.

In this new era, much prior work dealing with notions of movement gained new relevance, as did the notion of art as object. For the casual observer, it could seem as though the "advance detachment of

---

10   Breckinridge, C. R. (1900). Speech of the Honorable Clifton R. Breckinridge: In Southern Society for the Promotion of the Study of Race Conditions and Problems in the South, *Race Problems of the South: Report of the proceedings of the first annual conference held under the auspices of the Southern Society for the Promotion of the Study of Race Conditions and Problems in the South, at Montgomery, Alabama, May 8, 9, 10, A.D. 1900*. Richmond, VA: B. F. Johnson Pub. Co.
11   Swed, Mark. *Los Angeles Times*, April 9, 2016, http://www.latimes.com/entertainment/arts/classical/la-ca-cm-black-mountain-notebook-20160410-column.html.

a new form of life"[12] as, for example, the Surrealists saw themselves, had aged as a viable perspective, succumbed to use and fallen ill. Another movement passed away, as had Cubism, Fauvism, a string of artistic movements throughout the modern era before, and in their immediate wake, yet another split in vanguardist perspective began to open a vein of inquiry across fault lines well-documented, for instance, in Claire Bishop's accomplished, expansive tracing of participation and social practice histories (aspects of which, she also notes, were once also known as relational aesthetics). Operating adjacent to and in resonance with dance, movement art, and at distinct remove from any such centering on market (*oikono-mos*) value, these outgrowths may seem to align in the sense that much of the intent has been specifically to manifest interventions in thought, and in honing ideals for how best to interact and improve participation in advancing the ideals of equality.

My ideal for this first in a 3-volume reflection on all this history is in part to retrace the project I've set out for myself, and I see the focus shifting with each of them, starting with the reflection in this first book, much of which centers on avant-garde dance and performance, but that begins where I first decided writing had the best chance of affecting some sort of social change when I chanced on an interview with Kurt Vonnegut that originally appeared in Bridge, the journal I launched in 1999. In it, you can read how well he set the bar for me, one I recognized as thoughtful in the midst of so much pain and apathy in the world. In that conversation, these themes of policy, law, of violence and fair treatment in society and in life were questions that shaped the self I wished to echo, rooted in its most profound themes.

They will also frequently percolate back up throughout the

12 Taylor, Charles, *Sources of the Self: The Making of the Modern Identity*, Cambridge University Press, 1992, p. 471.

3 volumes, of course, but this represents my reintroduction to it in personal time, as a manner of description. Value systems are easily appropriable for industry use, and social practice has been a useful tool for much educational institutional mission, such that new departments have been established by very capable artists and educators. However, if art maintains any claim to "social relevance," how exactly, given these kinds of impasse into institutionalization, should we define it? Indeed, the purpose of all this does seem as if "from the beginning, the number one problem of modern social science has been modernity itself."[13]

Modernity clearly contains the seeds of Postmodernist claims, for instance, in the expressions of eros as a kind of discipline, and social ordering of form. You don't have to avoid protesting its inherent lack of contiguity to acknowledge that today, reality continues to endure new shifts, tumbling across media variants and spectrally endless thought-enclaves to effect, often divide and define both conscious and unconscious reflection. Against these backgrounds of artistic foment, as the historical avant-garde began to see its approach and *rapprochements* appropriated by and subsumed to the interests of neoliberal ideals of cultural cost-benefit motives, its practitioners could only watch as it was ultimately absorbed by neoliberal culture industries to serve the very ideals it originally stood as a bulwark against. Much of which, of course, was motivated by the grip of nostalgia for an avant-garde "blasting those who are corrupt, inept and evil,"[14] as Richard Schechner recently wrote in *Performed Imaginaries*, now severed from its social relevance and reduced to endlessly "repeating itself."[15]

It's this variant of what we collectively refer to as the "art world"

13   Taylor, Charles, *Modern Social Imaginaries*, Duke University Press, 2004, p.1.
14   Schechner, Richard, *Performed Imaginaries*, Routledge, 2014, p. 28.
15   Ibid, p. 28.

that has prompted its disavowals by important figures in it in protest of its corruption, a protest that took place alongside widespread earlier calls for regulation of its markets. Still, the art world remains largely unaltered despite much protest, and much recent outside social progress. As Nato Thompson described the difficulty in an interview in *Hyperallergic*, it's openly known that many "benefit greatly in the art world from neoliberalism."[16] In that same interview, Thompson makes the case that the majority of those participating in it are "people loaded with student debt or [who] basically can't afford to live in their apartments"[17] to distinguish between its implied neoliberal patrons and those pursuing artistic interests. Inequalities sustained by the institutions of art. Despite that standard of measure, and peculiar to much of the writing assembled in this volume is a seemingly endless search for the articulation of conscience, how it manifests in the work, often even as simply an expression of modern malaise. Each of the 3 volumes in this series of *Perfect Worlds* also thus represents that rare thing in so much academic research: evidence of field work, that is, in support of *Illegitimate Art*, a separate monograph I'm currently writing on the shifting structures of how new art forms are forged in relationship to these powerful socio-political, frequently ideologically-rooted oppositional forces. Those strains that branch off into the kinds of fascistic notions I've sought to offer some paltry frame have roots in a profound sense of hubris distilled with fabulist self-delusion, a state that philosopher Abigail Rosenthal describes as an attempt, by putting oneself into the shoes of a believer, for instance, in Nazism, as a person who believed they could

16   Vartanian, Hrag, *Curator Nato Thompson on Politics and the State of Social Practice Art*, *Hyperallergic*, Oct. 25, 2017. https://hyperallergic.com/407599/curator-nato-thompson-on-politics-and-the-state-of-social-practice-art/
17   Ibid.

" ... take the vital force that we sometimes call 'creativity' under his human direction, knowing it to be a great, even at times a decisive force in human affairs, he proposed to control the spigots, turning them *on* and *off.* His belief was that the creative force would not abate in any event, but that preeminence in creativity would belong to whoever got control of the force's stoppage and release, and constructed the channels through which it could flow. [...] The Nazi believed that national preeminence extruded from unquenchable natural sources of vital energy. Thus, one could stopper the flow here or there domestically, damn up the spring waters of other nations, and still leave the natural sources themselves to surge unabated."[18]

In this tug-of-war between radical ideology and imaginary, the modernist project to ascribe these values artistic form provides us some sense as to the battle lines of progressive reform, and the role of artists in it. Who else may be most influential in expanding the boundaries of equality and mutual self-respect, addressing society's social ills and pointing out corrections to the social imaginary, than artists? Our "unacknowledged legislators," in the implied abhorrence to violence of its most progressive practitioners, to those things that make "living together" more difficult, more violent, and more impossible? Drawn from personal life experience, artists are arguably most successful across many definitions of value and norm when they manage to transmute our shared daily experience into questions, in its exemplar, of this enduring branch of inquiry. Much protest activism, which takes a similar approach to personal politics as a reflection of shared experience, often foregrounds an aspirational dynamic of masses organized around shared political ideals. In an era of "Russiagate," understanding the influence of these forces on the social imaginary seems not simply critical, but

---

18   Rosenthal, Abigail L., *A Good Look at Evil*, Temple University Press, 1987, p. 217.

a central question for the preservation of our highest human ideals in the face of statist interests that would happily pry them away.

This series of research volumes, then, began to emerge as a way to share the notes I've been taking on these subjects, a way to disseminate and hopefully affirm evidentiary standards of the social sciences, urge new inquiry into how we forge connections between imagination and reality, and their powers for influencing one-another. I've enjoyed the vicissitudes of serving that aspiration, and the ways it has helped unearth new sources for art-making in the places that exist outside the "time out of mind"19 of our current art cultural movements, not unlike how art typically lags behind, but delineates how it may actually serve to prompt or respond to social progress, or that which it might "be in aid of."

19 Taylor, Charles, *Modern Social Imaginaries*, Duke University Press, 2004, p. 84.

Kurt Vonnegut [20]

How did you come up with doing this radio broad-
cast on WNYC?

> I have a friend at WNYC, Marty Goldensohn, and
> he's got me in on a couple of other things, covering
> the Republican convention and that sort of thing.
> So, he was paying me a call and he said they'd like
> to have these little spots to drop and here and
> there and would I make some? So I did and I had
> this idea of talking to people, so I thought that
> was okay and these things have all been run on
> WNYC. They're just little brighteners that they
> drop in throughout the broadcast day.

How did you come up with this idea of talking to
people in heaven for these broadcasts?

---

20 This is an edited version of an interview that originally appeared in the *Bridge v.1
n.1*, released in 2000. It was conducted on the occasion of the release of his *God Bless You,
Dr. Kevorkian*, which was written as a benefit to radio station WNYC. In both, he wrote
imaginary interviews with significant historical figures from throughout human history.

Well, that's what I do for a living is sit around and think up neat stuff.

Heaven seems like an interesting choice of subjects ...

Particularly since I'm the honorary president of the National Humanists Association.

Yes, and so the comedy in the book is so compelling, a comedy of accidents, and particularly the section on Newton.

Yeah, that was fun. Oh my God! He discovered practically everything there was, his two big ideas.

He's trying to discover the composition of the tunnel to heaven in the story.

It's a part of life and a part of the universe he's never thought about, this spiritual stuff.

You think there's any chance of him eventually discovering its composition?

Well, he has all the time in the world there, he's got all eternity and, yeah, well Shakespeare would help.

Yes, you actually reference Shakespeare in here.

Right, well where it says they're "trading innocence for innocence," from the *Winter's Tale*. A beautiful description of sex between two people, between two men or between a man and a woman or two women, whatever. In this journey it is trading innocence for innocence.

I'm very interested to ask you about the journalism aspects of this book, I pick up what feels like reporting in your books at large, and too in this book. How do you think about incorporating these journalistic aspects into your writing?

Well, that's what my training was, I worked for the Chicago City News.

I'm actually calling from Chicago.

Well, the news bureau was going to go under, and apparently was rescued. I don't know what the current situation is, do you know?

I don't, actually.

Well, the Chicago City News Bureau was a tripwire outfit for all these newspapers in town when I was there, so I was out there all the time around the clock and every time we came across this really juicy murder, or a scandal or whatever, they'd send a photographer and a reporter to cover it then

they'd run our stories. So, that's how I could have
a gig and go to university at the same time.

Wow, really?

Well, I was a graduate student and was mostly
working on my thesis, so I could make my own
time at the library. Well, back in my generation —
I was born in 1922 — you went to college if you
wanted to be a writer or write for the newspaper.

Yes. I read somewhere that you wanted Billy Pilgrim
to be played by John Wayne. I have to ask if that's
true.

Ha ha, no. That's somebody else. I would love it if
he had, though.

Hm! Have you ever met him?

No, but I'm sure we would have gotten along fine,
he's just an actor for God's sake. You know, Char-
leton Heston is just an actor.

It's just a job. Right, but do you think it's possible to
effect change in ourselves without doing real harm? I
was reading a take on your writing that said that per-
sonal change, according to your oeuvre, was achieved
by turning inward. I don't know how exactly they
phrased it but, it was a matter of personal change, a
matter of changing our personal natures.

Well, if there's a way of enriching your soul, and you so encounter some people that have very rich souls, and others who haven't done much with their souls. One way to enrich your soul is to practice an art, not for a living but simply to enrich your soul. Perform a piece of music or write a poem, or write a whole book or a sentence, or whatever. Paint a picture. Dance to the radio. All this enriches your soul and in the age of computers, computers are doing more and more for us all the time. So, they're cheating us out of the experience of becoming. You don't have to become anymore, just wait to see what Microsoft brings out next year. So I think people are so taken with this stuff so much that they'll become quite uninteresting.

Then they'll have to turn to other people. How formative or influential would you say your experience was at the University of Chicago?

A lot. You know, my father said I could go to college, but I couldn't study any whimsical stuff. If I went to college I had to study something practical and so my brother became a chemist and studied chemistry. So, they decided I too would become a physical chemist. I had no gift for it, what I did in college. I'm glad, because I know something about science. But I also know what it's like to be at the bottom of the class.

That is the trick.

> No, but I think all these experiences are good because I had no talent for science and I found what it's like to be the dumbest kid in school and also, when I remained a private first class, that was a good experience too. Because I was literally qualified for officer training school but all they needed was people to carry rifles. My entire division was wiped out, which was the hundred and 6th division, it was college kids. Privates and PFCs were all college kids.

That's all they needed.

> When I thought about doing this interview I think I thought about my grandfather, who was a Purple Heart recipient as well. He was captured at the Battle of the Bulge and I think that a lot of people my age — I'm only 28 — I think they feel a real sense of identification with people my grandfather's age. The shadows of the wars they went through. I'm not sure why it's such an easy connect.
> Well, it's so theatrical. You know, the Nazis were pure evil and whoever designed their uniforms was a theatrical genius. And the German cause was pure evil, that's all there is to it. I don't think there's been another war like that.

No, I hope there isn't. But when I was thinking about

my grandfather, it wasn't because of the Germans so
much as it was … he knew what it was like, he'd been
on the bottom rung for awhile.

> Yes, I know what it is like to be treated like shit.
> First as a private and then as a prisoner of war.
> Then, it was the Geneva Convention that deals
> with good behavior in war time — privates have
> to work for their keep. No other rank has to, not
> even noncoms. Corporals, Sergeants don't have to.

It's tough for me personally to relate. I haven't been
in the military, the closest I have to that experience
is the social ranks in school, who gets lifted up and
who gets beat down, and people trying to learn often
get the private level.

> Well, at the same time, I was at the top of all my
> classes at Cornell, except the mandatory music
> course we had to do, or the history course. But
> also, I was a big shot on the *Cornell Sun*, so I was
> being read every day. I was writing for significant
> New York papers, not connected to the university.
> So yeah, I was a big shot on campus, and writing
> a column every day.

When you first started writing these interviews, were
there people you thought of that you didn't end up
talking to?

Well, other people. When I started doing this, one guy said, "Hey, you've got to interview Clarence Darrow. Hell, he practiced in Chicago. Clarence Darrow not only represented labor organizers, he represented the Illinois Central. Yeah, but I'm proud of the Middle West. People like Darrow, and Eugene V. Debs. You know, Vienna is so proud of Sigmund Freud? Well, the Middle West ought to be proud as hell — Ohio, this is — that it was the home of the founders of Alcoholics Anonymous. Its saved more lives than psychology ever did.

I was just taking a class in the psychology of addiction, and this was a part of the history.

Well, the guys who founded Alcoholics Anonymous were inspired by William James' *Varieties of Religious Experience.* Which I happened to read, incidentally, when I was at the University of Chicago in anthropology.

Do you visit your hometown Indianapolis often?

Yeah, fairly often. I'm fond of the city and have friends there. My family used to be important merchants there. They founded a hardware store, Vonnegut Hardware. They came over, my ancestors came over at the time of or shortly before the war, one ancestor came over and went back for the rest of the Vonnegut family. But anyways, he founded a general store there in Indianapolis, Clemens Vonnegut came over from the north of Germany, immigrated, and actually it became a chain of hardware stores, Vonnegut hardware store in Indianapolis, and that sort of faded away, largely because I think of the tools coming in from Asia which were good, and much cheaper. Anyway, the trade connection to the Vonnegut Hardware store, and there's a Chicago connection on this. The Iroquois fire, do you know what it was?

No.

It was a theatre, the Iroquois Theatre. Caught fire and theatres were a huge business in Chicago at the time. They piled up at the doors, they couldn't get out. So, private Vonnegut and a couple of other guys invented the panic bar, which is that bar they use now in all public schools and all theatres, so if someone slams up against the doors, what happens? It flies open. That's the panic bar, and actually my family need never have done anything else to justify our existence here.

Right, well they saved lives.

Yeah. Well, it must've saved a bunch of 'em.

That's interesting. I'm actually from Fort Wayne, and you obviously have a very strong connection to Indiana.

I'm critical of the public school system, which I
hear isn't any good there anymore.

No. Not in Indiana.

How were the schools in Fort Wayne?

Oh, it was a process. I don't feel like I was made
ready, that I was prepared at all. Now, I've kind of
gotten out, at college.

What did you do at college?

Well, I'm still in college, at Northwestern.

What do you study?

English. When I graduated high school, I took five
years to try and do some writing, and then I ended
up in Chicago.

And you're happy for doing that, I hope?

I am. You're going to think I'm curious, and I hope
you don't mind me asking something so radically
off-topic but in a recent interview, you were toying
with this idea of Hammurabi and I guess you were
talking about —

— Code of law. —

Yeah. And what you said about Hammurabi.

There are two really radical inventions in the course of human history. Eh, one was $E = mc^2$, that matter and energy are somehow connected, and the other is "forgive us our trespasses as we forgive those who trespass against us." This is a radically new idea coming from Jesus Christ and, of course, embedded in the Lord's Prayer. Before that, revenge had been utterly reputable and had been mandatory. It still is. You know, if somebody disses you by God, you're going to get even if you're any kind of a guy or even a woman. Jesus forgives our trespasses and forgives those who trespass against us. It was a radically new invention and what had been done before, the code of Hammurabi, which was "an eye for an eye, a tooth for a tooth," was actually trying to cut down on the extent of revenge. You could only injure the other person to the extent they had injured you, you can't go haywire and kill their whole tribe. But, anyway, so that's it. Hammurabi was really trying to make revenge more reasonable, and Jesus said it's a bad idea. Of course, members of my profession — and if you're a story-writer, yours too — make revenge reputable because it's such an easy way to write a story. You start with a guy, somebody shot his mother in the back, and so you don't have to wonder what makes the guy act that way. And as soon as he shoots the other guy's mother in the back, well, you're satisfied, and that's

the end of the story. It's an easy way to tell a story.
Turn the reader on and turn the reader off.

A little too easy.

It's too easy, but we keep doing it again and again
and again. Particularly the cowboy story. The guy
drifts into town, and he's looking for the guy who
shot his brother. So it's an easy story to tell, and
that makes revenge seem reputable. Of course you
get all these people who don't know the difference,
and they'll beat the shit out of you or kill you.

Where do you think we can find writing these days
that raises the experience of ordinary people to an
epic level?

Well, there are masterpieces on television. After
all, we are the human race so we'll produce media
that's appropriate to the technology of our times,
and there are masterpieces on TV, particularly
Homicide. Of course, it's almost like the revenge
story in that there's a crime that has to be solved.
But it's more of a mystery. But I have seen epi-
sodes of *Homicide* that you can only watch in
reruns now.

I've seen a couple good ones.

Some of them are lousy, some of them are utter
knockouts. It's sociology and dialogue and all of

it absolutely first-rate. But most of the plays that people like so much, they were sitcoms. You put a couch there and a coffee table in front of it and a staircase going up the back, it would've been a pilot for a sitcom. You know, a masterpiece will pop up every so often because writer's just can't resist if they're really on a roll writing something. I remember one episode, oh boy it was hard. You ever watch the *Mary Tyler Moore Show*?

Uh, yeah! I did.

One episode was perfectly marvelous, it was a magical play. It was a radio station — or was it a TV station — but, anyway, Chuckles the Clown was in town with the circus and in the parade, an elephant stepped on him and killed him.

Oh, really?

And, actually, before this episode we'd never heard of Chuckles the Clown. And the men were making these coarse jokes all the time, these wry jokes about him and Mary Tyler Moore was getting deeply offended by the coarseness of the men. She couldn't see this was their own way of dealing with it. And then at the funeral, when the men were sitting there, very serious, Mary Tyler Moore started cracking up. And that's as good as any short story Mark Twain ever wrote. Ink on paper doesn't matter anymore. Used to be that even with a short story, you could hit a home run with three men on and everybody'd be talking about it. But

> people don't focus on short stories as much any-
> more as they would have before television became
> important.

Yes, or flash fictions that you put on the internet and
are meant to be read in two seconds.

> Well, that's all right. And what I find is, as I'm
> traveling from town to town, I travel around to
> universities five times a year, ten times a year, and
> what I've found in every university town, there's
> a local arts paper. People publish poems, print
> drawings, or short stories, and with no thought
> of making money, but doing it because it helps
> their souls grow. But I think with computers, as
> they become more and more interesting, people
> become less and less so and their souls will be
> starved. People are no longer becoming.

It's important to find a way out of that.

> Sure, you retreat. Get your own gang. You got a gang?

Sort of, but they're all kind of doing their own thing.

> What do they do for a living?

Oh, let's see. I have one friend who just started going
to medical school and a friend who is just finishing
up school and he wants to write but he's not sure.

Well, you have one. And the world headquarters of radio comedy and radio drama used to be Chicago, WGN. World's Greatest Network. You should know that about Chicago, it's what was coming out of there, as opposed to what was coming out of New York or anywhere else.

I've been wrestling a lot with Chicago, and only really recently feel like I can get along with it. I think I should probably finish school first.

Well, hang out with Steppenwolf.

The theatre?

Yeah.

Are you happy with the play they did for you there?

It required such stagecraft, that we didn't publish it because no amateur could put it on. A complex production. Anyway, they're purely Chicago. If you want, they're celebrating their anniversary, I can't remember if it's their 50th or something else—

Oh, it's not that much, 25th maybe.

— Okay, 25th then, but anyway they asked me to make a contribution to the book for it and if you called them and asked for a copy to see what I wrote about it, I'm sure they'd give it to you.

Thank you, Mr. Vonnegut. Those are all the questions
I have.

> Well, you've got my number give me a ring again
> anytime you want.

Jenn Freeman (aka Po'Chop) [21]

Your practice comes out of the burlesque scene, and
has migrated from there into other disciplines. How
did that all come about?

Before, I had been predominately in the burlesque
scene. After putting myself in certain spaces where
I didn't feel safe … 4in burlesque cabaret shows,
audiences aren't coming to face of any of the things
I'm trying to deal with, they're not interested in
having that conversation. They want to be enter-
tained. They want simple, surface entertainment.
They're not interested in examining sexuality, let
alone black sexuality. Let alone asking questions
about what some of the stereotypical views are
in a nightlife setting, know what I mean? They're
there with their date and they want to see a pretty
straight-forward show.

21   Originally published at *Sixty Inches From Center*, December 14, 2016, http://sixty-
inchesfromcenter.org/movement-matters-pochop-aka-jenn-freeman.

Right, they don't want to look under the surface and
challenge their own assumptions.

> Right. I think I've been fortunate enough that, for
> the most part, my work has still been accepted in
> those spaces among a lineup of people. If you have
> one, I'm most likely the only black person in the
> show and my work is very confrontational. I'm
> not letting them get away with this, we're going
> to process this, for the most part.

So, when was that moment for you that you saw this
shift taking place in your work?

> I don't know if my work has changed so much
> as gigging — gigging has slowed down for me.
> I know I don't need to be out in the nightclub
> scene doing my Black Panther piece. When I first
> started, it was kind of fun because those are the
> spaces, those are the audiences that need my work
> the most. I came to Chicago to go to Columbia
> College, studied dance and fiction writing and I
> didn't finish. I came to the city from a very small
> town in Missouri. Then, moving to Chicago and
> going to a big liberal arts school was like a Life-
> time movie. Imagine, that was my life. For a long
> time, I felt like the bottom had just been pulled
> out from beneath me. I also came out as gay, so
> there was that whole thing with my family when
> I was 18. Pretty much the summer of my fresh-
> man year. I came out to my parents and my dad

was a minister. I grew up in the church. My thing
when I came to Chicago was to study dance to
become a missionary. I, honestly, don't think I
knew what liberal arts meant. Had I known, I don't
think I would have gone to Columbia. I would
have gone to a more conservative school. But I'm
not complaining. I'm very grateful that I did go
to Columbia. But so, when I did come out, my
mother pulled me out of school —

Oh wow. They flipped out.

Oh yeah. And also, my first relationship was with
an R.A., so my mom kind of saw it as the school's
employee had manipulated me and it turned into
a whole thing. So, I dropped out entirely. I tried to
come back on my own, but it was like —

How do you do that?

Yeah. Everything that I had known was completely
gone. So I just spent 3-4 years drifting around
Chicago, just plowing through it. But then I found
burlesque, I had a couple of friends who had
started a troupe and they had to have been one of
the first groups who were a part of that trend here.

Right, there was a resurgence of burlesque, going
back into the '90's.

> I think I was drawn to it because it was all women and because of the fact that the person who's presenting it is in charge of all aspects of it.

Was this Jeezy's?

> At the time it wasn't Jeezy's Juke Joint. The Ripettes is what it was, and they had started after doing a fundraiser for a theatre company. This was seven or eight years ago.

From there to RDDI.

> Yeah. RDDI (Regional Dance Development Initiative) was this huge gift. It changed my life. I'm still trying to unpack and process that. I'm trying to figure out how I can give that gift back to the burlesque community. I'm still definitely thinking of burlesque as a form of storytelling. One of my acts is called *For the Record* and I come out in my own interpretation of a demure, high feminine figure and slowly transition into more aggressive, irreverent, very foul manner in which the final reveal is a bull dyke figure.

> This was all inspired by a trip that my partner and I had taken to New York to go and see a comedy show. I don't go see comedy shows but I guess in New York a very common thing to do is just come out and heckle the audience, to come out and do joke after joke like they do about whoever's in the

audience. And every single comedian, they'd come out and scan the audience and do jokes about every single person in the audience except me and my partner. So I thought about this and maybe one may have said something about my partner, you know, she looks like a lesbian, she's very butch. But just to think about that, what it means, that invisibility, for some reason they couldn't even see us, we're two women sitting at a table, very obviously touching each other and they couldn't even acknowledge the fact, in my brain at least, that we were lesbians. We're all humans in this room. If you feel it's appropriate to make fun of that dude over there, then why can't you make fun of the two obvious lesbians sitting in front of you? So that inspired that particular act. I think something I clearly struggle with is that, I'm someone who identifies as a lesbian and identifies as queer but I don't look like that so sometimes I want to push back against the expectation. There's this assumption too that just because I am femme that I'm automatically a bottom. I hate those terms, but sometimes I find them useful.

Yeah. That you can't switch or can't be fluid. And performing that act then in a typical nightclub environment.

Yeah, and I think that act is probably the most feminine I am on stage. Soft and demure. For me, I stay far away from demure, light foo-foo personas. My stage personas are usually very, very aggressive. I think when I first came into flirtation with performing, it was an alter-ego, kind of like a superhero. I allowed myself the space to be — I mean, I'm very shy. I consider myself an introvert. I didn't speak up for myself, so when I created Po'Chop, I wanted that space. I don't think it was intentional. Before I started performing as Po'Chop, I had 3 different names before I settled on it.

What were the other personas?

Oh God, they were awful. The first was Champagne Mystique — I had this friend who was in a sketch comedy group who hates burlesque so it was intentionally cheesy. And then the second one was Jenine Se Qua.

Wow.

Yeah, wow. Right? So once I settled on Po'Chop, I knew that was right. And I've done hundreds of performances under that name now.

Your work is distinctly political, though you mentioned it bothers you how people can water it down. How do you feel now about the political context of the work you're performing?

It definitely informs what I'm doing. My preparation, the flow of the act. Even before #blacklivesmatter picked up, I was looking at how a lot of Black Panther members were murdered and arrested —

Especially in Chicago.

Yeah, especially in Chicago. So, in the act, I had always been getting arrested. So now I go through many different phases of getting arrested. And, I'm not sure how many people pick this up, but how the different deaths look like on stage, from broken spines to I can't breathe to incorporating some of the other iconic movements that other people would associate directly to that movement.

Do you think there's a more consciousness of the erasure and white supremacy than when you began performing?

For sure. And I think Jeezy's Juke Joint has helped that immensely, especially within the burlesque community. For sure. I think Jeezy has been one of the spearheads of doing that in terms of visibility and bringing people up with her as she climbs the burlesque ladder. She's been really good. I know for a fact that she's referred me to several other things, which has definitely helped. I also think that's another reason I've been trying to be pro-active about the spaces I do perform in because it

> is charged. And, it's also — I'm not just revealing my body, I'm also revealing something that's way down deep inside of me so it's really easy for me to get my feelings hurt.

That and then the violence around black bodies and the uncertainty about the audience.

> I already don't feel safe living in this world, but then going into another space where I'm going to feel a whole other level of unsafety has been — yeah.

That, and then there's the whole gendered aspect.

> It depends. If you're going to a burlesque show, the audience is going to be predominantly female. But if you're going into a nightclub setting — I'm thinking very specifically about Untitled — it's going to be a very male-driven environment. And I think there's more money in that building in general, so there's going to be more privilege when it comes to women's bodies.

What?!

> I go into Untitled knowing I'm going to get touched by a stranger, at least 3, every time I perform. So now I don't really do that place either.

But if you're coming up, that's what you're going to expect.

I tell my students to say no. And the burlesque
community just formed a board with reporting on
sexual harassment about certain spaces. So there is
that. I also tell my students, if something happens
to say something but don't go there again. If you're
going into a space, use your intuition. We're not
getting paid enough, you're lucky if they're offer-
ing you $50. It's gotten a little better, but there's
a ways to go.

Ayako Kato [22]

How did you first become interested in dance as something more than an activity purely for enjoyment?

I practiced ballet from age four through nineteen in Japan. In fifth grade, I started to go to a more vigorous ballet school lead by Kimie Sasamoto who had been a prima ballerina at Masahide Komaki Ballet Company and danced with guests such as Sonia Arova and Nora Kaye, and also in *Western Symphony* and *La Péri* choreographed by Roy Tobias in Japan. She is renowned as a choreographer, and the first Japanese who received the International Award for Choreography at the Fifth International Ballet Competition and the first Japanese judge for Prix de Lausanne International Ballet Competition. She had also been in New York as an exchange fellow and had the fortune to visit George Balanchine's rehearsals.

22 Originally published in *Newcity*, August 8, 2016, https://www.newcitystage.com/2016/08/18/free-style.

Because of those experiences and influences she was carrying at that time ballet was more than enjoyment from the moment I entered the school.

Yet in the true sense, I would say, it happened when I returned to practice modern dance at the MFA program at the University of Michigan. During the first year, Mary Cochran, former Paul Taylor Dance Company dancer, was a guest artist and teacher in school. She asked us, "Why do you dance?" and I remember the moment of lifting my answer hidden in my unconsciousness. My answer has been edited over time to be precise, if I write it now, "I dance to express the dignity and the beauty of life." Mary's mumbling to herself after observing the rehearsal of the super aerobic piece by another group of casts was also very memorable, "If you don't kill yourself, it just makes you strong." Upon returning to Japan, I started to perform and committed to begin my career as a professional dancer and choreographer. Since then, I have been working hard, thinking that if people spend time and energy to perceive my dance, I have responsibility.

What makes your particular dance practice distinct?

I perceive dance as representation of energy. Human bodies are conduits of energy and our movement is a visualization of the intangible energy and our will. My practice is to express the internal to external and external to internal force which creates various phenomena, incidents as well as physical objects in the space. To physically represent this force through movement, my dancers and I prepare through somatic exercises which internalize our awareness of the body. In that sense, my focus is not creating steps or some movement sequence. Rather, I am interested in perceiving principles in nature and presenting the origin and nature of movements to realize the entity of being and share experiential moments. In that sense, I advocate to apply the idea of butterfly effect and mirror (and reverse mirror) image on human relationships and our relationships to nature.

My current pursuit is reverse reflection, against immersing myself into classical ballet for fifteen years with a focus on Western culture and competition during the highest Japanese economic growth period in the seventies and eighties. While I was away from dancing, I was influenced by the Japanese haiku poet Basho and by Taoist Chuang Tzu. Practicing Japanese tea ceremony and flower arrangement, I inclined to understand the philosophy of Tao, "The Way," which encompasses the path of Zen in artistic practice and action. Originating from an Eastern and Japanese view of nature, perceiving humans as a part of nature and nature itself, and recognizing the human

movements which embody "The Way" of nature
is an ongoing practice for me.

Nowadays, our mind can be so occupied by our financial conditions and materials among daily life. In the current economic system, without choice, humans can be easily occupied to spend our time and energy to make money, produce something to sell and consume. Then, it becomes easy to look over the fact that all those are related with how we consume our energy, life force, and what we use our lives and our life force for. By being aware of and noticing the subtlety and intricate inter-dependent relationship among ourselves and/or other lives, things, and elements in nature in the environment, I believe we can change something and move forward to a better direction.

I consider dance the art of being. Through dance, the audience physically and mentally experience the possibility of human transformation through the sonic and kinetic resonance with their knowl-edge, experiences, ideas and memories, and they can grasp new images of their life force.

Who are some of the most influential practitioners for you, and their key concepts, ideas, or approaches? How are or have they been critical to your own work?

I don't consider myself a butoh dancer. Rather, I consider myself a contemporary experimental dancer. Yet my experiences of taking workshops under Kazuo Ohno over three years, whose movement is deeply philanthropic and humane, made a huge influence on me in terms of learning that we need to practice by ourselves in order to establish something original, practice the best I can without thinking this and that, practice repeatedly until I gain the law of nature, the law of movement, or the truth of the movement. His advice and call of "Free Style! Free Style!" can still resonate in myself.

When I was into Chinese Meridians and working to activate the paths based on the five elements of nature: tree, fire, earth, metal and water, and move by sensing interdependent relationships, I felt I needed more scientific help based on Western anatomy. (Later, I found there are some overlaps between Chinese meridians and anatomical paths of veins, artery and nerves). I have been studying with dance anatomy scholar Irene Dowd the past eight years. Her Proprioceptive Neuromuscular Facilitation exercises based on anatomy studies and biomechanics truly helped me to work on my alignment, stabilize the center of gravity and freed my movement. In recent years, I am influenced by the idea of Tensegrity by Thomas Myers. This idea is to perceive the body as the holistic architectural, sculptural "tension + integrity" structure that skeleton and bones are coordinated together by elastic muscle fibers and myofascia. Myers states, "the actual skeleton the bones float in is a sea of soft-tissue. The myofascia acts like an adjustable tensegrity around the skeleton — a continuous inward pulling tensional network like the elastics, with the bones acting like the struts in the tensegrity model." And when I apply this idea on any relationships through movements, connecting with butterfly effect, moving solid, physicalized objects as skeletal bones and air as the medium or a sea of soft-tissue where solid, objects are taking place and related via something beyond the tangible facts. I am starting to integrate Irene's muscle specific exercises and Myers' Tensegrity concept together based on my classical ballet, modern dance, and Eastern movement — such as Tai-Chi and Noh Theater Dance — practitioner background.

Other than Kazuo Ohno and those scholars, artistically I am fond of works by Jennifer Monson and Crystal Pite from recently and I never forget the performances by Marcel Marceau, Jorge Donn and Maya Plisetskaya I witnessed growing up. I am also often moved by very sincere and honest experimental performances not only by veteran artists, but also by emerging artists.

Shirin Neshat [23]

Is this the first time you've been back to Chicago
since your 1999 premiere at the Art Institute?

> Yes, I think that's right, actually. It's been a very
> long time.

I think one of the big questions I'm curious to hear
your opinion on, as an artist who acknowledges the
political exigencies of your work, is what you think
of the Muslim travel ban.

> It's a very complicated subject, of course. I think
> the reason for political events in the U.S. is of
> concern for people like myself, particularly because
> I've had a lot of problems with my own govern-
> ment and its hard-liners; and to see that kind
> of thing happening in this country is not very
> encouraging because I always felt very secure and
> at home in the United States, and now I'm feeling

23 Originally published in the *Chicago Tribune*, March 24, 2017.

a little bit more shaky. You know, it even interferes with people who have immigrated a long time ago and now don't have a way back home, a sense of insecurity happens — "what will happen?" But I think, more than anything, I feel also like an American who's very concerned about if this country might be leaning toward fascism and all of these horrible things that none of us wants to happen. It's a great concern, I think, not just for Muslim immigrants but for all Americans.

You've spoken previously about how artists in Iran have faced "harassment, torture and execution," and I'm curious how you see this nationalist shift in America echoing that or not.

Well, I think the lack of freedom of expression is really key, and I have a feeling that that's what we're seeing in the last 18 or so months in this country, which was unimaginable that the freedom of expression would be reviewed or taken away from people the way. ... But of course these days Iranian artists are not at as great a risk of being tortured or killed because, at the beginning, earlier on even during the green movement, for example, we had very severe treatment of people who are openly speaking against the government. But right now in Iran there is more moderation. But really I think this is of great concern for artists, and for international artists, to see this same kind of thing that more backward countries are going through.

It's revealing that you point out the moderation in Iran right now, at a time when the far right image being constructed in the national dialogue is one in which they're threatening Iran with new sanctions, seemingly out of nowhere.

> Yes, this is really, really unfortunate. It's not helping. And to alienate Iran makes so little sense. You've never ever heard of an Iranian terrorist. Of course there has been conflict between the U.S. and Iran forever, but the terrorists have come from Saudi Arabia, Morocco and other places. But those countries are not penalized, so it's really targeting Iran in a way that actually serves to unify the Iranian people against the U.S. For so long, the Iranian people have been big fans of the United States, and wanted to make peace and have thought very differently from the government. But now the U.S. has really alienated the Iranian people. So it's very disturbing because, on a human level, it's such a bad decision to do what they have done to Iran. They should really look at the record of the Iranian people in this country, in the United States, because they are some of the most educated in business, and science and everything. So we have contributed so much to this country, and now for them to be penalized seems insane.

A lot of your work has investigated this nexus of faith, violence and ideology, an intersection relevant

to both American and Iranian cultural histories. Do
you see the focus of your role as an artist changing
in these new contexts?

> Again, a tough question! You're absolutely right,
> all of my work has always been about this dynamic
> between people and power, like governmental
> institutions, fanaticism, religion and mysticism, the
> more humanistic aspects of existence as opposed to
> it all. And I have to say as part of my talk (at the
> MCA) I wanted to talk about the transformation
> of my work and how it's changing and evolving
> — and yet all of these dynamics are still existing.
> I guess all I could say about what's different about
> it now is that I haven't been back to Iran for so
> long, I've turned a corner in terms of no longer just
> obsessing about the Iranian culture. I'm moving on
> to questions that don't just relate to Iranian society.
> My latest work relates to American culture, which
> I've been working on while I was in Egypt.

And speaking of these shifts, is the depiction of
women changing in your work as well?

> People always ask me, "Are you a feminist?" And I
> say, just because I focus on the subject of women,
> and I'm interested in the subject of women's strug-
> gles, does that make me a feminist? I recently gave
> a talk in Canada and somebody got up and said
> "You are a feminist!" I feel that women's points
> of view are naturally very different from men,

regardless of where they come from. I think our choices of subject matters have a way of breaking into our points of view on politics, religion — and are vastly different from men. But to just reduce them to these questions of gender, no I would hope we wouldn't. We usually don't discuss a man's perspective as a masculine perspective, we just say it's a point of view. I think while my work really deals with the subject of characters that may be gender related, it's from the point of view of a woman and often the story of a woman. But I think it talks about broader issues that happen to be in the experience of a woman. Obviously, that's because I'm a woman, and very often I think my work is reflective of my life experience as a woman, so that's how it's shaped.

Jamal "Lightbulb" Oliver [24]

What was it like for you growing up as a dancer in
Chicago?

I'm from out west—63rd and Albany, right
around Kedzie. I pretty much grew up over there
all through childhood and high school. At least
[until] my first couple years of college. Then, I
broke off and moved around to the east side. I
was everywhere, though, growing up. I was getting
into footwork and playing basketball. Growing up
around there you had sports, you had kids around
the neighborhood doing kids' stuff. I don't know
how it is now, I haven't been over there in awhile,
but then, everybody kick it in their hood together
and footwork was around. When I was a shorty, I
was the kid at all the family functions that knew
how to dance like Usher and Michael Jackson.

So you would dance at house parties and that sort of thing?

24   Originally published at *Sixty Inches From Center,* February 7, 2017, http://sixtyinches-
fromcenter.org/movement-matters-jamal-bulb-oliver.

It was local. Everybody would go to those [parties]. But nah, I wouldn't go to that when I was younger because I was going to school. [In school], there was house music, footwork and juke music—like they're playing now. But I came around like in the 2000's so, in the '90's there was juke music playing. When I got to high school I joined my first dance group—that was my freshman year. It was called Total Impact. That wasn't even footwork. It was pretty much a group of guys in a band—they were upperclassmen. They knew how to sing, they actually went viral on Facebook a couple weeks ago. They're known for singing on Jackson at the blue line. I started with these guys and they pretty much taught me dancing. After I joined a band during one show I tried footwork. It was horrible, but I [still] tried it on stage in front of everybody. They thought it was okay. I wasn't really in the realm of footwork, but I was just trying to see because I was known in the high school for doing it. I knew it was weak. It was weak to the people who were really doing it outside of my school.

I was like 16, almost 17 when I first tried it. I'd seen people doing footwork and if you were from Chicago that was just a thing to do. Know what I'm saying? There wasn't really YouTube in the 90s, but [when it came around] I started looking up footwork and [teaching myself]. After the first time I got on stage, I just kept building.

My sophomore year I joined a group outside of my school, a local community dance group called Alpha and Omega. From there, I started getting into my own style. When I was older I was taking the bus everywhere and making a local name around the Englewood and Oak Lawn area.

Was it a situation where you had mentors out of the community or whose work was inspiring your work in specific ways?

I didn't really have mentors. I was just doing it all myself back then. There wasn't really anybody trying to teach me anything. I think I learned a few moves from old crews [and styles]—like house. But I was pretty much observing and doing my own thing and people respected my style. I was always energetic and was always the first one to dance—always in the circle.

I joined a larger group run by Latisha Waters. She's like a old school footwork legend that used to be at all the parties at Union Hall and the skating rinks. She had an all-dance group called 3rd Dimension. I joined that group. It was funny because Nicole, founder of The Era, she was in 3rd Dimension back then but we just didn't know or weren't cool with each other. This was a very, very large group. Tish also had a tie to a larger group called Terra Squad and they were a battle group from back in the 2000's that was pretty much one

of the top groups that had all the legendary mem-
bers from back in the day. They had made their
own path. And Tish knew them. They came to a
3rd Dimension practice one day—AG, the leader
of the group, and Tyrone [Taylor] the president—
and I battled them. It was pretty much the three
of us versus AG and TY. At my first battle, they
told me about tryouts [with Terra Squad] and
went. There were so many people that came but I
was one of six who made it—I was pretty much
the number one pick out of those 6. There were
even people that were kicked out of the group
who had to tryout again. It was a crazy ordeal for
me to make it like that because it was extremely
hard to get in the group. But then once I got in
Terra Squad that was officially my first day in the
industry as a footworker in the larger industry in
Chicago. I was officially in it.

That same night, we went to a party. All the way
out west, we was in the 100's, all the way out south,
there was like 50 of us in the group and literally
killed the whole party. I couldn't even believe it
was my first day in the industry. There were fifty
people in one crowd battling during the whole
party. That was one of the memorable parts of my
life in terms of footwork, straight up. I went to
every battle and every event, making my way up in
the rankings through Terra Squad. I wasn't really
all that good, but I was getting better coming up
under AG, Speedball and all the other leaders. You

learned everything and was mentored by the whole T.S. and all the original members who were going through the struggles, going through the trials, going through the footwork and having to battle all across the city. We were taking the bus everywhere, still going to school, leaving school early just to go be a part of certain events. All kinds of stuff happened growing up being a footworker.

So that was how you came up in the Chicago industry, but then how did it make the leap to this international touring?

In my first year I was King of the Circle. That was big for me—to be a first year person, make it all the way to the finals and be competing. When I placed in the finals, it gave me a lot of respect from the community in Chicago. From there, I just needed to build my name. But at the time in Terra Squad I was one of the youngest members. They had it set up for me to take over Terra Squad and they were recruiting new members. It just so happened that they were recruiting after King of the Circle. I was trying to figure out what to do next.

Manny and Steve-O tried out for Terra Squad and they made it, too. It was funny because they were my age and everybody in Terra Squad was older than me at the time. So they were learning from everybody and me at the same time. They started doing stuff outside the group. We got cool because we were the same age and [we] started doing stuff together. They were 16 or 17 and I was 20 or 21? I was a lot older than [they were], but we got super cool inside Terra Squad. From there we just kept building.

[Around] 2010 or 2011 DJ Spin [told] me, "Man, you should get your passport and go overseas." He had been making music, making records and [had] already been traveling and pushing the footwork culture and music outside of Chicago. Their first large tour was overseas—as far as one with a record label—and they wanted to bring footworkers. I pretty much had been asked to come but still had to do all the work to raise the money to get a passport.

Michelle Kranicke [25]

How has dance changed for you over the years? It does seem as though you've always had an intellectual approach.

> I've always had an intellectual approach, absolutely. And I did, when I was younger, I would be inspired by things I read and I would set off to make a dance that was inspired by a book or a philosophical idea, but 9 times out of 10, that jumping-off point would really just go in a different direction, in a much more abstract, open investigative direction and as I've gotten older, as a choreographer, I've sort of done away with any kind of narrative as a jumping-off point for the work. I don't. It's much more conceptual.

25   Originally published in full at *Occasional Inquiries, Jan. 19, 2016, https://medium.com/occasional-inquiries/in-depth-amid-festival-s-michelle-kranicke-c717e5cdd04d* as part of the Movement Matters series, excerpts from which were also published at *Newcity*, Jan. 14, 2016, https://www.newcitystage.com/2016/01/14/unexpected-beauty-michelle-kranicke-bebe-miller-and-deborah-hay-talk-dance-ageism-and-the-experience-of-socially-conscious-performance.

It does seem like there's a lot of crossover. There has always been visual art, poetry, philosophical blendings or hybridizations of form that have lent new directions and new possibilities to dance. The question now seems: where do you go with that? It does seem as though your background in multi-disciplinarity is informing your perspective as well.

It is informing my perspective and I wish it would inform more of the art form's perspective. I was talking a little bit earlier about how dance theatre and dance, in and of itself, is abstract. You don't look at a movement and immediately understand what it is, because there's no language attached to it. So, from my standpoint, why even try to create narrative out of movement? Why even go that direction? Especially because, from a practical perspective, dance is a very poor art form. You have nothing to lose. There's no big cash bundle there that you're going to lose. You might as well just take the challenge. So I think, last time I saw you, we were discussing how I was frustrated with my own process about 4 or 5 years ago and I was also finding that I seemed to be seeing the same kind of re-organized steps on stage and I felt like the art form needed to push itself further. I started seeing a lot of performance, working through [performance art gallery] Defibrillator and I really felt like there was a gap there that could be mined and really allow dance to push to its edges a little more because it was safely entrenched in this place where it felt like it knew it could get an audience. And I get that, that's a frustration. Nobody wants to play to a house of 5 people. But I also think that dance doesn't have that big an audience anyway so why not jump off a cliff and try to see where the ending point is, where the gaps are, the edges where new ideas and new thought can arise?

Do you feel as though innovation has stagnated in the field overall, or is it just something you're seeing specifically in some performances?

I feel like it's been awhile since I've seen something where I thought, "Well, that's pretty new or interesting." I've seen a few things, but I think the form as a whole is kind of at this point of stasis where it's like, "If we do this we'll get an audience and be able to satisfy some earned income thing." I also think that it's so hard to stay in the form for a long period of time, that those sort of deep, intellectual investigations and the desire to cross disciplines doesn't really happen too much. I mean, not cross-disciplines with another performative form, like theater —

Poetry, graphic novels, …

Sculpture! Architecture! And so, it's funny. I'm working right now on a piece that I'm going to show several different studies from in this festival that will ultimately be part of a kind of larger installation work that I'm collaborating with my husband on, who's an architect, and who comes from the visual art world, and we're always frustrated when we go to see dance and there are props on stage and no one ever does anything with them. Or there's a big collaboration with some very well-known visual artist or architect and it's just this big thing on stage that people dance around, and I never really understood why that thing had to be on stage if you weren't going to actually actively interact with it. I'm not saying that's everybody, again, there are exceptions to every rule, but that's been my experience. So, it's interesting where the performance aspect comes in. There's a point where it's important there's a trained body doing this work, because if you're going to put the body in tension or do something with an object that requires an understanding of shape or form, or endurance, or in a specific place where you're in a position for quite a long time, especially one that's very technically demanding, then you need to have that formal training. From my perspective, and especially for this festival, I really wanted to bring in artists that were engaging in a critical way with a lot of pushing…engaging with this idea of expanding, figuring out how they were doing that. And sometimes, that pushing to the edge is simply forcing yourself to create a movement onstage where you're putting your body through the paces the way you did 20 years ago, and now you're 70. And putting yourself through those paces is going to be very different 20 years later. It's interesting because, originally, when I first got this commission, I started reaching out to all my heroes. I actually reached out to Meredith Monk who is celebrating her 50th anniversary year of being a performer and a maker and, of course, I couldn't afford her, and she wasn't available anyway, but what was great was that everybody was very gracious, everyone I contacted — all my heroes — all of them were gracious, which was really wonderful. But I got this movie of her where she remade Education of a Girl Child, she reproduced it 20 years later with the same cast and then there's a solo she does and in this particular film, you also see the solo as she did it in 1989, then in the 1990's and in 2008 and then you see her in 2015, and the thing that was so interesting about that was to see the very subtle distinctions and differences that happened to the movement as it was manifested in [simultaneously] a different, but also the same body. That was really cool.

What stood out for you as a signal moment, watching that, in thinking about your own work?

I'll tell you, it was really great to watch. What stood out for me was this command. Small subtleties within the piece. When you're young, you don't understand subtlety so much, but you understand how to eat up space, take up room, make the largest movement really large and the smallest movement really small. As you get older, you start to understand the subtlety that takes place when you go from one place to another and as you begin to understand that more and more you can bring in this command of each little step along the pathway in doing that same movement because it's not about going from point A to point B, it's about every little incremental place from point A to point B.

Right, that virtuosity.

Yes, but an expanded kind.

One that's more eternal … lasting, but internal.

Right. I work with my company a lot exploring this idea of internal versus external, inviting yourself to be seen rather than presenting yourself to the audience. How do you invite the viewer to watch you presenting yourself to the audience. It's two very different things. How do you navigate going in and out. Let's say you're doing something still and minimal for a period of 10 minutes. How do you manage all of those involuntary things that just happen to you and your body that you're so used to dealing with if you have an itch or have to sneeze, how do you deal with that internally while continuously presenting this idea of "I invite you to look at me now."

That more mentally and emotionally aware state you can get from life experience, if you're rigorously empathetic enough. Physical memory.

> Absolutely. You get it from experience, and practice and practice, and … practice. So all of the artists coming into the festival, I've seen all of them perform in one capacity or another. All of my heroes! There's sort of a tiered situation happening, in that there's Bebe Miller, Bob Eisen and Deborah Hay performing, some seminal figures that people my age and younger looks up at, and then there's myself and Sheldon Smith, who heads up Smith-Wymore Disappearing Act with his wife Lisa Wymore and there's Pranita Jain — they are more contemporary colleagues, so we have a similar kind of aesthetic understanding right now, and maybe the people that are younger than us look up to us, but we look up to these other 3. So, I feel like that's the interesting continuum. So, while someone may come to the show because they know Sheldon, maybe they won't know Bebe because they just don't. It's amazing what people forget. It's amazing how fast time is going. You know, my company members, they all missed the '80's. They missed it all. So all of my musical references, and even some from the early '90's, they have a hard time with. I love the fact that my heroes are here, but maybe it's also somebody's else's hero?

And I think it gives the public just…some way of

getting a handle on the historical contexts.

> Right. And I think it's important for the public to understand that dance is not just what you see on television, it's not *So You Think You Can Dance.* That's a great show, I'm not going to disparage or knock it. But I will say, it restricts the form and puts it in this very narrow bandwidth.

All the usual appropriations into popular culture.

> …And there's all of this conversation happening around the importance of making sure that everybody can see themselves on stage. And I think that's absolutely important. All ethnicities want to be able to see some body onstage that they're like "Oh, that's my body, that's my skin color, my sexual preference. That's onstage for me to witness." What's not onstage for people to witness is "Oh, that's my age. That person is my age." Because most of the time it's somebody who's 20–30 years younger.

Right, the youth cult in this country. Is that as common outside the States?

> Okay here, I'll date myself: when I was living in France in the '80's, it wasn't so much, but I don't know. I think it is now. Because of the global nature of our lives these days.

Well, and the attendant shift to a global market cul-
ture, with the youth cult manufactured in part by
people selling beauty, how Capitalism appropriates
that.

> Exactly. Again, we have a very narrow definition of
> beauty. What is beauty? So, even in the Dove cam-
> paign, where it's all "love your body," I'm like "Yeah,
> but it's not 60 or 70-year old women's bodies."

Yeah, people get trained to think of that as if it were
a grotesque. Which is a sickening idea.

> Yeah. And they do think of it as something gro-
> tesque. You know, I can only speak to cultures I've
> lived in. I've lived in France and, at the time I was
> living there, there was this very deep strong respect
> for older women as extremely smart and powerful.
> Again, whether that is still that way, I haven't lived
> there for a long period of time, since the mid-80's.

Regardless, the point is that in your work, you're
pushing back against convention, against these
self-destructive received wisdoms.

> Isn't that what art is supposed to do?

I want to ask people in visual art this question the
last so many years. Yes! Otherwise it's just entertain-
ment, isn't it?

> Correct. There's a great guy who set up a journal for teaching artists, and he always said, "Entertainment is what you know, art is what you don't know." And I'm always like, that is so true. If you know it, it's just entertainment. If you're confronted when you see something, if you're like, "Oh, that's weird and different —

Yes. Art should unsettle.

> It should unsettle. And unsettling doesn't have to be a bad thing. It just wants to make you say, "Oh, remember that not everything is set in stone. Things can be different and we should be moving forward." It's funny, as I'm reading Nietzsche again.

Great stuff, and most people don't pick up on the fact that his entire project is anti-nihilist.

> Anti-nihilist, absolutely. It's about finding your deepest aspiration and pushing to get there so that when you are really devoted, the suffering is worth it. If you really aspire to this thing and you really, really want it, it's where you want to be, you will suffer for it. And that's okay. People will always twist and misuse writings for their own personal reasons.

One of my favorites is "Ignorance is bliss." Do you happen to know what the original context of that quote is?

I don't.

In the original Thomas Gray poem, it's actually
"Where ignorance is bliss, 'tis folly to be wise."
There's a prime example of where Pop culture appro-
priated and twisted an artwork to mean the exact
opposite of what the writing clearly intended.

Ahhh! I have to say, I've come to philosophy later,
because I don't like not understanding things, so
I tend to avoid — okay … that sounds really silly,
because I don't understand what I'm doing every
time I go into the studio, and I'm perfectly happy
to grope around. I don't know what it is with lan-
guage, sometimes I just want to grope around. I
don't think I have a lot of philosophical influences
particularly. I don't have a traditional dance back-
ground particularly, either. I didn't go to college
for dance or follow that trajectory. I was a Politi-
cal Science major. I started off taking ballet class,
but I came to it late, I was 13 years old already
when I started. Then I left the country and lived in
Europe for a couple of years. So I tried to absorb
as much as as I could. So, I didn't come to dance
in this traditional way where all I saw was dance,
because I was never interested in just dance. I was
interested in visual art and theatre, and listening
to music and I played the piano for 13 years. I was
always interested in 13th century composers and
melody, harmony and rhythmic changes. So, I had
all of this soup of stuff swirling around in my self

before I dove into creating dance. And it never dawned on me that "Oh, you can't do this because that's now how it's done in dance," but then what happened was, then you get into the field and run up against the political, cultural, industry things. This industry that says, "well no, you need to go about it this way." And it's not overt, it can be very subtle. It's why I love the idea that you don't have a background in dance, but you're passionate about the writing.

Right, well, it's about the philosophical investigation for me, of ideas across art forms.

You have a strong understanding of visual art. I mean, dance, for me, dance is just as much a visual art. It moving, it's ephemeral. But so is so much visual art. There are pieces of artwork that I'll never see again because I'll never get back to that place.

I think that's what drew me to what you're doing initially, this attempt to add another layer to the world of dance, to expand and enhance it.

Let's just expand the conversation, because I think even with its practitioners, the conversation can get so limited and so tight, and territorial. You feel a little like, "Oh somebody's going to push those boundaries …" and people can get a little protective of what they've created themselves, and I think that's death for the form. Absolutely.

Pop will eat itself.

> My favorite Modern art story is the erased de
> Kooning. I love that. I love that this guy — and
> if you ever hear Rauschenberg talk about how he
> stood outside de Kooning's door, freaked out and
> knocking on his door and talking about how he
> wanted to do this — and then the fact that de
> Kooning was like "Yeah, sure," and then made him
> the most challenging, difficult thing to erase, he
> went through what — how many erasers? Like
> 50 erasers? But again, I think as an artist you have
> to constantly allow yourself to be challenged and
> keep growing, or you do become tight, and you do
> become territorial.

It's also this problem of insularity. It reminds me of
my ex-girlfriend, incidentally also a dancer, who had
that problem; she couldn't see the world from anyone
else's perspective, this escapist lack of empathy.
The consequence, of course, is a delusional culture.
Anti-intellectualism.

> Well, the thing I think is interesting is you can't
> continue to put yourself onstage, after a certain age,
> without expanding. Without being loose. You have
> to. You can't get tight. Because you'll find yourself
> confronted with things you can't possibly do any-
> more. But what I think is really funny — talking
> again, about expanding the conversation, and you
> go from big canvases to small canvases because

you can't physically do the movement anymore — like when we were talking earlier about Rembrandt's late style — I mean, that conversation is just never ever part of dance. I mean, maybe with Cunningham, maybe with some very few people. But I think that idea of a late style, or of shifting what you do, it doesn't diminish what you did before. No one thinks the early Rembrandts and the late Rembrandts, no one's like, "Oh those late ones suck!" just because of when he made them.

Well, that's always the sign of a true master, someone who has the range to change their entire body of work and reinvent themselves.

Exactly! So why can't you change yourself in your own body, why does it have to be so filtered? I think a lot of it is economics and the status quo. You know, "It's always done this way." Oh, dance is this. Okay, ballet is one thing. It's a very specific technique, it's a very specific vocabulary. But I have a friend right now who's trying to challenge that. She's trying to think about ballet differently. And that's a tall order. But I think it's really great. I feel like, with dance, if we can't do this, if there isn't this capacity within the performer, then the dance won't be a success. I think, as a choreographer, well, I've got this capacity to work with. This is what's up to me, to work within that narrow parameter and spread it out. Figure out how to work within that parameter and come up with the most creative — have you seen that movie *Wolf Pack*? It's a documentary about these kids that lived in New York on the Lower East Side, and they never, ever went out. Their father basically kept them in the apartment — for whatever reasons, fear of what might happen to them or this or that — but they got to watch movies. Their understanding of the world was almost entirely through movies and television and music. So, what they did is because they were locked up in their apartment — their mother home schooled them so they were very smart — but what happened is, they would create elaborately create or re-create these scenes from movies, for instance from *Reservoir Dogs* or *Pulp Fiction*. But of course, they're putting together their costumes out of cereal boxes, duct tape, markers and paint but I'm telling you, it's the most interesting, creative exploration because it's like "Okay, make reservoir dogs in this glass." How do you do that? I was watching this, and I thought it was so creatively interesting because they're in this very narrow hallway of what they could do, literally. So they expanded that in whatever way they could. And dancers are only getting more and more capable. There's so much technique today, you can't just be a ballet dancer or a Modern dancer, you have to be well-versed in all forms. Modern, ballet, West African, Hip Hop. I mean, if the choreographer wants to throw that in, and you as the practitioner, if you're young and want to work with a variety of different people, you

have to know those forms. But you know what,
sometimes you can have 20 different ingredients
on your counter and come up with a really crappy
dinner.

I think, for me, while choreography is great, I also
take a lot of inspiration from visual art, from film,
the nouvelle vague and Godard, who I think is
amazing. A lot of the Japanese directors, there was
just a Wim Wenders festival I went to. Especially
when filmmakers are experimental and they're
younger and pushing boundaries, what I love is
looking at what they do with limited means, and
then what I think is interesting about a figure like
Godard is, here's this well-revered filmmaker who
drops out of making film for a long time and then
he comes back and he's working in video. And
his newest film, which was a little bit hit-or-miss,
but what I liked was he was like, "I'm going to
experiment with everything. 3D. A little GoPro.
A little handheld," …and he did. And while the
whole thing didn't necessarily gel together, there
were parts of it that were just amazing, and it's
about pushing those boundaries. So, I find film
really inspirational. Visual art. Sculpture.

So, really it comes down to how the Popular concep-
tion of dance is insufficient to the form.

I guess I'm going to admit that, yes. I'm always
surprised at the lack of knowledge of other art

forms out there. I want to say it's about the gaps, the gray area between the two. I think we talked about the fact that "Oh, you're a dancer. Oh, you're a performance artist." When Zephyr was doing a lot of its performances at Defibrillator, people would say, "Oh, you're a performance artist now." And I thought, "No." Why would we be performance art now, just because we're in this space? Just because we've chosen to show something in a gallery setting. I think it's so reductive, I think in the States, and it's Capitalism, it's so intent on defining, "Well, this is this. And this is white and this is black." And you know why? Because people don't know, they want to know, and they want an answer. You'll go to Heaven if you're good. You'll go to Hell if you're bad.

Right. People think I look like a girl when I'm wearing nail polish and a dress, but I'm not. And I'm intersectionally informed enough to rest confidently in my cis-male identification. Hopefully, this cultural moment we've been having, where ambiguity's been getting ushered in as a more accepted part of our everyday experience, will take a more permanent hold.

It is. I'll be interested to see how that translates artistically because I think ambiguity is being ushered in, and people will accept different people's choices about how they want to live their lives as long as they never have to talk about it. As long as they just pass on the street and it's fine. I think art forces you to talk, it forces that visceral reaction, that gut reaction where people can either think, "This makes me really uncomfortable." Discomfort is something that people never embrace. I don't like discomfort, but especially if I'm seeing something artistic and I start feeling uncomfortable, I think, "Let's look at this again." I'm the masochist, I'll look at it again and see if I can find a new understanding of it. So, to that end, I don't want Amid to make people feel uncomfortable — it's not set up that way. It's set up to make people expand their ideas, expand their understanding and, when something's abstract, they tend to shy away from it. Because they have to bring their own meaning to it and they don't want to. They want to, they want to be told. If you want to be told, you can go watch TV shows, which seems to be all the rage. There's 7,890 million different kinds of TV shows.

The only thing worth watching lately has been The Cosmopolitans, Whit Stillman's pilot. They sit around and talk about literature and philosophy the whole time. All his work is like that, it's the best.

Jose Santiago Perez [26]

You're originally from Los Angeles, correct?

> Yes, I'm originally from L.A., a first generation
> immigrant from there. I lived in L.A. until about
> 2002 and then I started to move up the west coast
> and right before moving to Chicago in 2013, I
> spent about 10 years in the Bay area. So, in terms
> of movement and dance, my first exposures were
> in the Bay area, so Keith Hennessy, Ralph Lemon's
> work in San Francisco and even just historically
> too, there's Anna Halprin.

Right, especially with Halprin this approach sort
of rooted in nature, as opposed to the Cunningham
conceptualist, interdisciplinarity of the New York
School. I've been tracking your work awhile now,
and remarked on seeing some of the sculptural work
you had up recently at the International Museum of

---

26 Originally published at *Art Intercepts* as part of the Movement Matters series,
Sept. 15, 2017, http://www.artintercepts.org/2017/09/15/movement-matters-an-inter-
view-with-jose-santiago-perez.

Surgical Science. You approach art, movement and performance as intimately connected, and it was that intersection in your work that drew me to want to learn more.

> Yes, I was having this conversation with Colin Pressler, the curator there [at the IMSS], about how my focus was starting to shift away from the live element of those sculptures and having the performance itself withheld from the audience and just having the artifact. And thinking about the climate we're in right now, and I haven't really made the connection, but there's something about this particular embodiment that I'm in right now that feels a little more vulnerable than usual that I've been doing. It's hard to talk about because it's really complicated, but I can only really talk about it from being inside the performance and having a certain kind of gaze on my body, as a sort of brown, effeminate male and there's something sort of difficult to manage around that. I haven't fully figured out my position right now but it feels like a way for me to retain some agency around how and who gets to gaze on my body and who gets to consume that and I kind of feel like withholding it a little bit, I get to retain some agency. So, how do we talk about performance-based sculpture when the performance itself is withheld? It starts to get a little bit tricky, and so when it came to how I would proceed at Defibrillator, that sort of aspect came out a lot more.

You're referring to your upcoming night of perfor-
mance at Defibrillator with UK-based artists Gary
Winters and Claire Hind?

> Yes, Joseph Ravens reached out and Mark Jeffries
> at the SAIC performance department is putting
> together a program to bring them in, so I think he
> was trying to pair guest artists with recent alumni.
> They'll be showing work in the main space of the
> gallery and I'll be showing downstairs and there's
> this Thursday evening programming they just
> started doing called Tiny Garage and we'll all three
> have open studio during that time. So for that, I
> think I will have my body in the space and available
> and that's a shift, it's a shift that I'm working with
> right now, it's a little clunky, I'm not really sure
> where and how that'll work out but I feel like it's
> a way to try and trouble performance a little bit,
> the gesture for me given the kind of conflicts in
> the world we live in right now, I feel like I'm in a
> protective, survival mode. So if I can exert some
> energy and agency over how my body's consumed
> by whom and at what time, even if it's the illu-
> sion of agency or a fantasy of empowerment, I'm
> willing to grasp that and, just in terms of myself
> — I'm incredibly shy as a performer too — there's
> a way in which this kind of gestural way of working
> allows me to honor this way of being in the world
> too, which is weird, right? Because I know there
> are a lot of shy performers and it's like, "why are we
> even working in this mode anyway, then?"

Well, sure. Part of it is the reflection you get from
the introspection and that then you need some way
to put it out there into the world?

> Yes, and I'm also interested in this idea of perfor-
> mance not being the product itself, but a mode of
> production, a process of making.

I love that. You've read Andre Lepecki? I'm very
steeped in these kinds of ideas in my own work about
the expanded field of dance as choreographic prac-
tice, with the work product being the interaction
that takes place.

> Yes, when I was at SAIC and Lin Hixson really
> turned me on to Lepecki, and especially one short
> piece called *Ghostly*, about movement and spec-
> trality which resonated with me because that was
> the kind of work I was doing then.

It's interesting and, frankly, Lepecki is writing often
in dialogue with a lot of theorists in and around Chi-
cago who are writing and thinking about dance, but
also about movement and performance art in a larger
sense which for me is rooted in the historical avant-
garde. I've written a lot digging in and finding points
of connection across the disciplines about these ideas,
the work of Susan Manning, Sally Banes, both of
whom Lepecki refers to repeatedly, and lately you
have Elise Archias. These kinds of thinkers, fostering

these locally-rooted philosophies of the art forms
that define its international outcomes.

Yes, exactly.

Karen Finley

I'm really looking at how new art forms are made,
and looking at the history of how art forms are legit-
imized or de-legitimized by the social imaginary.
This history of the social imaginary as this concept
of how people think about themselves and society,
and there's a tension in that notion about norms and
values and how they're expressed through ideology.
As I'm conceiving of it there's this whole tension that
goes back through Nazism and degenerate art and
that then threads up through McCarthyism and of
course directly then to the culture wars, so your work
is situated at a fulcrum point in the history of that
research I'm doing into how ideology intersects with
the imagination. Artists in general contribute greatly
to the discourse that happens around the range of
available ways we have to imagine ourselves, and
what I'm trying to get at is the social consequences
of that, how certain artists are either suppressed or
silenced. Or how it connects with other strains of
thought that may be homophobic, transphobic, or
racist and how those responses are coded into this

oppressive dialogue that happens as a result. So, your
work, looking at the '80's and the Reagan Era is really
emblematic of where that conversation went, and has
continued to go. Clearly, people saw your work as a
threat in this sense.

> I think, for my life of creating work for 40 years,
> it is impossible to be thinking that this era of
> suppression or censorship only landed in the '80's
> and then in the '90's, but continues today. I think
> I'm offering alternative views, because there's the
> dominant narrative, which is that the artist creates
> work that goes against the State and then offers
> an alternative and then the artist is depressed or
> silenced. Then you have this reaction, legal reac-
> tion, and then things go on, it's a series of steps.
> So when you ask me your questions, I'll probably
> give my responses as two-part answers, one from
> the dominant perspective and then an alternative
> perspective.

I think, really, starting out, I don't think you saw your
work as a threat to any particular individuals when
you were making it.

> Oh, yes I did.

Oh, you did? Could you elaborate on that?

> Well, I think *threat* is the wrong word. I have to
> go back to what I was thinking about performance

and looking at performance in the type of work
I was doing. So you have to go back to that era
and looking at historical times, and looking at
degenerate art and McCarthyism, and so putting
it into that context I started creating and — being
in Chicago, I started doing performance work
— during the Vietnam War era. It came out of
protest, and protest art. For example, thinking of
Abby Hoffman levitating the Pentagon, or if this
is Northwestern, I participated in the demon-
strations that were happening at Northwestern
as a high-school student. So I came out of those
times, and part of those times were thinking about
economies and disrupting the market, or of having
access to the arts so that the idea was performance
as a way of creating forms that were disruptive to
the art market. That I would say was being dis-
ruptive, so I was entrusted with creating work that
would be disruptive.

There's this whole historic thread that runs through
the avant-garde that's about pushing back against
that kind of bottom-line, or instrumentalized think-
ing. Were you thinking about it in terms of the
historical avant-garde or you just picking up what
was in the air at the time?

You know, I was trained in the arts, so I had an
awareness of the artists that were working before
me, Yoko Ono or Yves Klein, and so you're a part
of the world or making of the world at the same

time, there's a simultaneous combustion that was occurring. And that was what was happening with me, I was part of the world and creating work that was responding to the world. So, thinking even about histories of artists who would come through Chicago, too, historically, whether that was going to be Joseph Beuys or Yves Klein, or thinking about the Chicago Seven and then the NEA4, but thinking about resistance and how artworks formed resistance. At that time, the work I was doing was not going to be in institutions but was thinking about — during this new NEA and about public art and the public sphere, in the engagement and breaking down of the social strata but also inherited wealth in relationship to art making and art collecting.

Performance art during that time hadn't been around very long. Did you see this as more experimental, or did you think you would have this kind of effect when you were starting to work with it?

I did not feel as though it had been short-lived. It was a small enclave, but the art world as I knew it was a much smaller community than what it is now. I think that's just because of the educational reach and the art markets, but when I was growing up studying the arts, it was looked at more as being a deviant or an outcast, just in terms of how one lived in order to be an artist. So, in deciding to be an artist — it just depends — I grew up in

> Chicago, I went to the Chicago Art Institute as a young person and there was an urban, liberal support outreach for [living an] artist's lifestyle. There was N.A.M.E. gallery or these other galleries, but it was an alternative world that seemed to have a knowledge that, always within society that there was a world of an alternative. So for me, and I think I'm unique in that way, other people won't feel that way, but I thought I was part of a historical tradition of artists, of a Bohemian lifestyle, that there was an alternative that had been going on probably since the beginning of time.

Right. Yeah. I've been looking at the historic avant-garde going back at least to the beginning of the 20th century, and its variants in Afro-Caribbean and other cultures, and thinking about — it's modern, right? So they're all these different types of responses that crop up again and again, almost of a cyclical nature, and I think artists are all too often at the forefront of that, but it's often about this line of respect for difference in people. I'm thinking now about the work you've been doing, looking back on your writings about HIV and recently at the Alphawood Foundation and the work you were doing there. I think you were very vocal and cognizant of the need to defend people at the time, in the face of what I think were very anti-gay and homophobic things that were happening.

> The reality is that I might have been censored but that my status in society of my whiteness, and

my gender, the way I present myself and where I landed on Earth, all put me in a place that when I enter a room, I expect to be served. So that's why the conversation needs to be shifted because — I was censored, I was oppressed, but in looking at it, how oppressed was I? Yes, I received death threats. Yes, I went to the Supreme Court. But at the expense that many other people who were not even recognized. But in saying that, I have an awareness, and that's why I would be speaking up and out because it was safe for me to do so, or more safe than for other people.

I want to ask, is the work you were making at the time, was it in response to personal experiences you were having — you stated pretty publicly that it was, but I just would like to unpack that a little more in this context.

Well, the unpacking is that if in speaking out, and if you — the dominant position is in looking at how I was oppressed, and to an extent yes — if you want to compare my career to other careers, and then looking at the scale of success, one could easily do that. Although I volunteered for much of this. I have selected, self-selected, certain areas for my career. I have a scale of integrity or authenticity, and I can afford to do that, find my station or my status. I was aware that when, it's not really even just an awareness and knowing this, I need my place with my whiteness in my education and

> what I could do, and I was pushing boundaries,
> but it was at the awareness of knowing that friends
> and family and colleagues could not. And even if
> they did, I would be, just because of whether it
> was the media or various other reasons, I exhibited
> certain — whether be it a talent or a storyline, that
> made it legible. So, I was legible for the media, or
> for politics.

So you're saying there were others out there who just
didn't have the social access required to obtain the
legitimacy that you were enjoying?

> Yes, I think we can use legitimacy, but it can also
> be very gendered, too. I don't know if that would
> be happening now at my age, with my sense of
> idealism, the desire and the way I presented myself,
> my education, even coming from the middle of the
> country. You know, I had long hair; the way I pre-
> sented my gender expression, that was allowed and
> that isn't the whole story, but it definitely is part
> of the story and that has to be understood when
> it comes to artists. Especially gay and lesbian, and
> artists of color, that I had that extra — I can't put
> it in an amount, but let's just say for argument's
> sake 10% — I had that extra 10% coverage and
> that means a lot when you are so marginalized,
> when artists are so marginalized.

I've heard you talk a lot about your awareness that
you were enjoying, these kind of privileged aspects

to this just didn't translate in terms of other work.

> Yes, but I think it's important to be — when people are looking back at these kinds of situations — because I don't feel that people understand that enough, I don't think that — you know, I think that I was shallow, I think I had a shallow understanding when this was happening, and that's the reason why I wanted to take it to the Supreme Court, because they didn't think that I would have the strength of character to take it to the court. You know, that I'm educated and have the strength of family, because usually so many artists are disenfranchised from their families.

Yes, it's a matter of having a sufficient support system.

> Right, and I had that support system.

Do you think it changes minds or do you think it just stands as a record of history, as I've heard you talk about it a few times in the past?

> I have two responses. I want to give an example after giving a response to the ways in which institutions silence artists, and so I'm going to get back to that in a minute, and how to navigate or work with that. I think I was part of a movement in an era when artists were making responses towards political and societal change.

> It was at times metaphoric, and I can send you a recording of my *Written in Sand* piece — it was a direct response, but it was poetic, and advocated for a change in policy. And we have had changes in policy, whether it's gay marriage, we still have woman's right to choose, we still are fighting and divided in terms of policy and so I'm proud of being part of that.

So it is a very structurally an activist approach for you?

> Yes, but I see it as — I know you came to the talk [at Steppenwolf], but I see it is this role of artists as historical recorder. So I see it as accountability of witnessing, of response and that's what I consider my role, or what I can do. That's the recorder, the filtering and reading and translating.

It seems to me there's this thing that happens in a very cyclical way in which an ideology impinges upon art-making, depending on the political winds, particularly with white power, when something like the Trump era comes along and pushes this message of, "We're going to have this national community again, and exclude the world and exclude others we don't like," then there's this push and pull that happens with each generation, it seems to me, and that the artist has a role in that. So, part of the question I was just asking is how much this just has to happen with each generation — are we making permanent changes or is this just something that always has to happen?

It's not a math problem, it's a lifestyle. I was just thinking about my friends, and before Facebook or social media, you as a writer for instance would be included in that community. Poets, musicians, community and people would hang out together. I'm sure you remember that, you would drop by houses and visit people and just hang out, and that would just be going out and spending time and, that's one of the reasons I wanted to speak to you on the phone, I read the article you wrote on my Steppenwolf appearance, and I wanted to have a conversation with you. So you know, that's just part of the fun and integral to human experience, you know just listening and hearing and then having a response, that's what performance is about, too. You have these rituals or rooms where people are coming together whether they're taking a shower or whatever, and thinking about their premeditation towards coming together in this moment, and it's a relationship between intimacy, public, and private and I get the juices going. we're having this conversation now, and that's part of what that is. There is a world, there's a difference between the world of artists and institutions, and it is the private spaces, the intimacy and the relationship of these poetic spaces and the personal sphere with the public sphere — and with institutions, you're thinking about the public sphere trickling down into the personal.

This is really an interesting question. Performance

is at this place where it's now being brought a little
more into the history of art, into the museum and
a little more, historicized and taken away from its
social moment. Do you see that as being the case?

> I think you can be taken broadly, because it's a
> genre like discussing music or discussing paint-
> ing, so it's a genre but there can be — I think
> there is significant work in institutional spaces,
> and I appreciate those spaces, but where I've had
> to, in talking about institutional spaces, when
> talking about the oppression that's taken place in
> my career, is institutions or certain funders have
> suppressed or stop funding me, so I couldn't push
> it to that next level. So that was a psychic expe-
> rience, and I think I've spoken about that a little
> bit. I've had to come to terms with that and not
> be bitter, and to return to look and see things but
> that is kind of the price of doing the work that I
> do, that there's certain artists that are allowed in,
> that become neutralized within the institution.
> I mean look — maybe it was fantastic, but was
> it really political work there? When it becomes
> Hollywood, does it become what happens then
> — what are those relationships? I mean, I work
> in institutions, but those are things I think about,
> and juggle, and consider all the time.

I think about other artists who work in similar
or parallel modes, thinking of perhaps a Carolee
Schneemann, and I know they're very aware of

pushing back against particular conventions and society, and then having various degrees of reaction to that work in public and it becomes that question of to what degree institutions have a role in supporting the work of that artist. I think your work in a way pushes back against these institutional barriers and then through that out into the public.

> Yes, so there is the tension. I think Carolee Schneemann's work, she has not received her retrospective at MoMA and she should. She should have a retrospective at the Guggenheim, the Whitney, and I don't understand why that hasn't happened.

I think it evidences the problem: she's making this very feminist work that's about empowering femininity and womanhood, and I think that is being responded to in a very misogynist way, for instance, when she describes how people would characterize her work as simply narcissistic, and not valid. So then, you can't get a call back for 10 years because there's this dialogue that goes on around your work which is about bigotry out in the culture. So if we're talking about this erasure that takes place out in the culture, whether you're talking about people of color or others, there's this invisibility that takes place and I'm really talking about it in terms of artists who may be making work around these social concerns and in the case of Schneemann, if you ask why she hasn't been given it, it's because she's been put under erasure, in that same sense. It becomes a convention-setting standard that becomes a norm out there, and I think that your work, I think you fought back against that in a very powerful way through the court system. I look at that court case, and I don't think there's any question that it was simply vacated to avoid the question of decency in the case, because there were clear instances in which the NEA was banning, for instance, the depiction of homosexual eroticism, and other types of depiction of sexuality in a way that I think was homophobic, transphobic, whatever you want to call it, and so this is a very interesting question that goes to how our institutions function.

I think you're right. I hear you.

I think that becomes a challenge when you're working in performance art now, that when you bring it into an institution you're working against the background of those problems. So, I think the question now is, how do you balance the interests of making art, which I hear a lot of people saying these days, you know, "I'm going to channel my resistance into making art." And when I hear that, in my head I hear myself thinking, "How will you make an art that's *effectively* resistant?" So I think this question is central for me in my own art-making, and probably on the minds of a lot of people who are making art, how are they doing it in a way that makes it effective?

I don't think that you can predict it. I don't think
you can in creating work, and that's something
I've become very appreciative of, is that one can
never predict what work will then become focused
on, and what work will be ignored. That, one can't
predict. Even with my career, I just did my show
at Steppenwolf, but I didn't really get any press or
attention for that work, so it's really interesting to
see where people are going, and what's happening.
I think that the work I did for Alphawood this
past weekend was really extraordinary. I kind of
look past how many people are there, or who's
speaking, because I look at building a work and
creating a work, and seeing its significance, and
that's what keeps me grounded. I made some deci-
sions, and I'm lucky because I work in education
and there are some ways in which I can do that
work that I can't through other means, through
books or whatever, and I have supported myself
through my artwork, but I don't do that now. I
would have probably had to have been in exile, and
that was offered to me, you know, move abroad.
And I considered it, moving abroad, being an artist
in exile.

Sure, Beuys wouldn't set foot on American soil while
the Vietnam war was going on.

Sure, well. I considered it. I thought, well, if it's
based on the strength of my work — many artists
have had to go abroad and come back, Baldwin,

Beckett, there's a history of artists, people who go abroad. I actually had invitations, people inviting me to do that, but I thought in order to stay with my lawsuit, and in order to stay with American policy, that I had to remain here unless things got to a certain point where I had to — I'm not going to be proving that much of a point but it was never a situation where it was like Pussy Riot.

Where you were imprisoned, or something like that.

Yeah.

Ginger Krebs[27]

This performance has been in development for some time for you, at least a year working with your current ensemble, but also in various stages of artistic development prior. Can you tell us how this journey began and then evolved for you, and what its conceptual development has involved?

Yes, this piece has been in progress — not continuously but with the dancers, about a year. I guess, of that year we worked really intensely for six months. There was a gap. But yeah, we worked from the very beginning in May and then showed a work-in-progress in the dance studio and then I built this big, tilted platform that the whole performance happens on. I built that in June and then we did a first quick test run in July and we just really had 2 weeks in the space in July. Then we had a long gap in our rehearsal process and

27 Originally published at *Occasional Inquiries*, Feb. 2, 2016, https://medium.com/occasional-inquiries/in-depth-ginger-krebs-the-future-of-humanity-the-annihilation-of-now-b05261f846a7.

then we were hitting it hard in the beginning of November for the show. So now this big platform is rebuilt for the fifth time in this space. I'm pretty excited about how it changes the feel of the space. I built when we first rehearsed in Uptown then tore it down and moved it and built it again in the Cultural Center dance studio, and then I moved it and built it again — but I'm pretty excited. I mean, you can imagine how the movement might be, what it might look like, but it's really taken time to deal with the physicality of the thing, how it messes with your sense of gravity. I'm kind of pleased, it's a lot of work, but it's not like we could practice on the flat ground.

Part of it has been practicality. All of the artists I'm working with are established in their own right, with their own careers, so some of it was working around their availability. This piece seemed to require a lot of time to interpret the visual — the piece started at an even more of a visual way than some of the past projects. I made a bunch of drawings — to call them paintings is probably to elevate them — but prints, and works on paper. In the period before I even started working with the dancers, I made a bunch of images and I feel like I've been working with this set of ideas for awhile, even though I don't think of myself as a drawer or a painter, but I've been interested in a kind of dispersed field of visual composition — such as when I think of a digital image, I think of it as

comprised of many pixels, I think of the energy in
that image as dispersed, versus a kind of ... when
I think of the weight of the body, I think a lot
about, visually, in contrast to this dispersed field
of pixels, almost like a cartoon, a kind of Sharpie
line around the body that says "this lumpy thing
here is a body because I say it is, because there's
this outline around it."
So it's a transposition.

I think I'm interested in the mismatch, in the way
bodies are depicted on the screen versus the feeling
of what it is to exist in a body and what it is to have
to make effort to move. As opposed to the kind of
weightlessness — bodies onscreen can have shape
but not weight, and they can kind of move like
everything's easily reversible and so, even though
this started out as a kind of visual inquiry for me,
almost like the impossibility of them being both,
of being like a cartoon-y kind of outline and this
things sort of energetic background. I made this
link — and maybe many people have, I don't know,
that the kinaesthetic experience of moving, when
you're not trying to make a move look a certain
way but you're trying to open up your sensory field,
it has more this quality of tiny little nerve-end-
ings that, for me, there's a little bit of a correlation
about how I think of this pixelated field and this
strange correlation between the digital world and
the physical world of weight and dimensionality.
Before I even worked with the dancers, there was

a lot of reading research, movement research on my own and then making a bunch of images, for some reason was important. I would say that the progression, in some ways, it has been similar to other processes. In the sense that stage one is often just generating a ton of material and, initially I also felt like, with this particular group of dancers, they all have quite a bit of training. Other groups I've worked with, they don't often have a lot of training, except the anomolous one here or there, and so it actually took more time at the beginning to almost articulate what the systems are in this world. And I think the piece addresses networks, systems, multiplicity and data in this way. This idea that we're getting used to seeing ourselves from an aerial perspective.

The French call it the *pensee de servol*, the "bird's eye view."

There was this amazing documentary about drones at Facets that I went to go see and it was all about putting drone footage in the performance, because when I think about the bird's eye view, a lot of it is vertical bodies transposed onto the horizontal, there's a lot of planar stuff that messes with your spatial sense, but it tends to have a flattened screen kind of dimensionality. A drone pilot shot all this footage of me out on this landing strip. Stage 1, with the writing, it was all of these things basically trying to relate to these things about speed, forward momentum, this drive for efficiency, which to me connect up with economic systems, political systems, even more personal stuff like discipline. I feel like in my young life, as with a lot of these dancers, kids are constantly being told to hurry up or slow down, sit still, whatever, so we tried to think all these different ways that speed plays itself out in the world. So it's very non-linear, but developing these constellations of materials that were interesting — I think about how Cheerios link up and become little rafts in the milk — that's sort of how the piece starts to build. So stage 1 was really that: "Hey, here's a lot of stuff!" and because the dancers are really skilled and can remember a lot of complex things, I could play with things like phasing in time like I'd never really been able to work with before. Just developing those systems took awhile because I wanted there to be a fair amount of complexity in what we were doing.

When you say phasing, do you mean transitions?

No, I mean like [composer] Steve Reich or a warping of time, say a dancer gets behind by four counts, everybody else gets behind by four counts, then maybe they speed up and catch up again, I wanted in time to almost recreate that feeling you get — I'm thinking of a horse race, but not a horse race — it's almost that feeling you get when there's no stable center, but everyone's shifting forward to back in relation to one another, those kinds of time are very persnickety and mathematical. So that first phase was playing with a lot of those things, and the second phase was really short, really we just rehearsed for two weeks and it was the first time to see what it was like being up on that platform, also the first chance for Joseph Kramer, who's generating sound for the piece to see what the sound could be like. Up until that point I had always just built my own soundtracks — and then there was this long break and November, we got the systems, we know what the world of the piece is, and then really trying to get much more specific about the roles of the performers and how they as individual, particular human beings relate to the material and draw out the humanness in contrast to all this really systematic, opaque and relentless objectivity. Because, while I'm interested in systems, I don't want to make a piece that's formal. I mean, yeah there are many important, formal things but I guess I'm wanting, in the piece as a whole, almost like the humanness of each performer to appear and then get absorbed back into the system. So, November especially was this time to find out what exactly could they feel really strongly about in terms of … in a way, when you have all this kind of tight choreography, you're asking for a lot of obedience and you have to be well-behaved and execute the things 4, 5, 6, 7 times. I'm really interested in and concerned, you know, I would never want to just show a piece that was, "Oh! Interested formally in patterns and space," I'm really interested in what happens to human beings when we have to adhere to these things, or this idea of an authority imposed from outside, how our bodies absorb that, how we cope with it, and when we fight against it. This last phase has been about trying to open up and find where the humanness is in the world. Then, most recently, in December, this piece has required a lot more precision, even more than past things I've done, and we're also working with a fair amount of video imagery and constantly scrolling data presence in the piece, and trying to work how all the elements come together and not be redundant of one-another, cancel each other out, and so balancing all that is totally exciting to me, but it takes a long time.

It's a lot to compose through these cascades of evolving experiential understanding! It seems operatic, all the different range of associations, including recurrent ones like speed, which seems as though it emerges as a kind of trope? Do you think the piece is Futurist or informed by Neo-Futurism?

That's so funny that you say that. Yeah. This is like a confession that I'm not sure I wanna … everything that I set out to make cutting-edge always has a retro-Futurist feel to it. No matter what. With this piece, for some reason, the '80's — I've had to become way more educated about

120   PERFECT WORLDS

what performance art was happening and what
was happening in alternative theatre at that time.
Not that I want to make it … I can think of a lot
of things that are way more contemporary than
that, but when you say Futurist —

Oh, this notion integral to Neo-Futurism of the
necessity to push back against technology, in some
respects, against dehumanizing social behaviors.
Narcissism, nihilism, the near-sociopathic lack of
compassion implied in instrumentalizing other
human beings for almost casual appetitive or bot-
tom-line purposes. For me, it evokes this lack of
empathy that seems so pervasive in our technolo-
gized social relationships to one another.

So, okay. I'm definitely not interested in making
some blanket statement about technology, but I
do feel like I have big concerns — I wonder if
this shows up in the piece or not — to what ends
technology is used. Who's using it and for what
purpose? I was reading a lot of Paul Verillio in
the early stages of developing the piece, and being
really interested in the idea of how, as the ability
to execute things becomes exponentially faster,
it's almost as though the algorithm that makes
something happen, happens faster than the human
mind can decide, and I guess that's like an example
of where my concern comes in. And I think we're
at that point right now where things can get put
in place way more quickly than a rational human

being weighing pros and cons is going to be able
to operate. So I think speed in that way could
potentially be a [negative].

Yes, this ability to render things, relationships, in the
physical world without judgement, and intentionally
building on this almost self-destructive potentiality.

Yeah, and it's almost like me looking at my own
[behavior], but I've learned somehow to priori-
tize efficiency almost to a ridiculous degree, just
in terms of my upbringing, of what was the most
important thing: getting the job done quickly and
correctly. I learned that was way more important
than the way you treated the human being you
did the project with. It's the way Capitalism filters
down, there's this idea, you're going to maximize
efficiency, on some level to make money for some-
body, but the way that filters down and affects
interpersonal relationships, that's deeply troubling
to me and I'm guilty of it. I wanted to make this
piece, in large part, to question these things that
I see myself doing. And sometimes it's a funny
thing, sometimes I can laugh at myself noticing,
"Ooh, wow! It's really important you shave 30 sec-
onds off your travel time!" Sometimes it's funny,
and sometimes it's really upsetting. It's like impa-
tience with other people, it's harsh.

So, in a way, for you, this is about slowing things down?

It's funny. When I was proposing to make this piece, I set myself up with some personal challenges about seeing what would come up if I were deliberately inefficient. This is a real departure, but at the beginning of thinking about this piece, I had this residency in Wyoming and I just decided I was going to see what it was like to get from point A to point B without using the highway, but going through cattle country with fences, to know what it would be like to constantly be diverted, take the path that's set up for us to go most efficiently. I was trying some things like that, and when I was talking about the November phase of the project, one of the ways to try to … if the world were a piece of all of these systems, has either been about being influenced by coding and loops and constant forward motion of something. And even this sort of harsher quality of correcting … there's one section in the piece in which two dancers are interacting I hope in a way that's disturbing but not in an immediately nameable, but one person sort of adopting the passive aggressive role, like "I'll yield to you, but according to my own agenda," and the other person in the more managerial role, trying to get somebody to adhere to the thing they want them to do. Anyway, these sort of power dynamics are there.

It reminds me of [novelist] Jonathan Franzen's essay on how technology has begun to alter the scope of our relationship with selfhood. Code as an imposition of the engineer's own perspective on others. When you get a multiple-choice in a range of settings that's presented in that predetermined way for you, your range of available actions are self-limiting based on those available options.

> Totally! You're constrained, which is a kind of a consumerist constraint. In contrast to something like fascism, where there's an obvious bad guy, what's interesting to me now, I don't know if this is post- post- whatever … nothing's very clear, power's always underground and it's always shifting.

There's certainly a clear nihilism that motivates most struggles over power. In interpersonal relationships and otherwise.

> And I think that there's the absence of a clear sort of anchor. Zizek is another guy I like a lot, he has this example of the Fascistic Father tells their kid, like, "I don't care if you like it or not, you're going to go visit your grandparents." But now we're like, "Do whatever you want." On the face of it, we're given all this choice but actually the imperative is still there, but it's not owned up to directly. Anyway, there's something connected there. The piece as a whole, I'd be curious to hear if it strikes you this way, but in a kind of perceptual vertigo, which I think the inclined plane has a lot of effect on that, but I think it's also what we're working with about the gaze and vision and not having an

anchored place to look? Some people, without any sort of suggestion on my part, they had said they were kind of sick from viewing some of the earlier versions. I was interested in this idea of nothing ever stopping, and even this notion of a constant undertow which I hope that the scrolling text is going to help to establish that quality but it's also really built into the choreography too. Instead of having a horizontal flat floor and architecture that tells us that we are here in this space, this constant orientation toward — whether it's your phone as you walk down the street or Google Glass, where you're seeing the diagram of the space superimposed over the space — and that we're doing this as we move through the space. I'm really interested in what that makes possible, or what that shifts?

I think it's really fascinating how they're using code to do things like scientific modeling, it's extrapolated and set to the actual physics, so much energy exerted by the pull of gravity per square meter, modeled after the actual physics for things like the Mars missions. That sort of thing.

Yeah. This idea, I think about it in relation to opacity, and this will be our focus in our training the final weeks before the show, after tomorrow's nuts-and-bolts blocking, at a certain point the face can almost blur into the rest of the body, just be a part of it, but at other points, I guess they're like characters that emerge. But they're not just characters because, for instance Elise, one of the dancers, part of her vocabulary has sort of been inspired by this notion of the anxious pet that wants to make everything okay. There's this sort of very disturbing undercurrent of violence happening between these two other performers and Elise is in this role as…you know, how a pointer is sort of looking to something outside and then orienting herself to that thing, then trying to decide … looking at the audience and seeing "how is the audience taking this, is it okay with them?" and then sort of scoots over and, I don't know if you're a pet person, but I've had dogs and when there's some fighting in the family they'll sit, thinking that "Oh, that's made them happy in the past," and so little by little, this sort of opaque, blurry systematic-ness, how these individual human beings cope with the relentlessness, maybe even the boredom of that, I almost want the specificity. Their roles, their characters are really influenced on many hours of process with these particular human beings. But I'm not interested in oh, "Now it's Elise's moment to be herself!" I'm not interested in that. So, in that sense it's not freeform improv, like "I'm going to express myself now," it's improvisation but we've worked long and hard to come up with a vocabulary of really charged things that hopefully in the moment of performing, she can really connect with and feel dynamically connected to. So yes, for the audience one of the things I hope is that they see…I mean, in one's dream scenario, that the audience can see something of themselves. In the struggle of these performers to emerge a kind of systematic driving forward of "be productive, be productive," that they could maybe feel the poignance. On the one hand, it's a physics things but, for some reason, for me, when I think about the antidote to this sort of world that is more and more influenced by abstract information, I think of two things: human effort and work. And for me, the effort of going uphill, it's very poignant for me to watch these bodies going up over and over.

Certainly; it recalls Sisyphus.

It is…I don't want it to seem quite that bleak, but there's something noble and beautiful to me about how human beings try over and over, even when it's misguided, it's effort. And for me, with this piece, where action is so much the point of departure, the physical work of this thing is something that feels somehow … I feel like I can trust it in this way that I'm not so sure about … and then the other thing, which is a little different, and we've worked from this in rehearsals, what is the sort of opposite of all this speed, quickness, hurry, faster and this notion of patience. Patience in-particular not as a notion of just going along with things, not just mellow and going along with things. You mentioned in your email that you're a parent?

Oh yeah, 11 years and counting.

So yeah, you know about this. I feel like parents know about this. It's the painstaking work of calibrating your speed to the speed of someone else. And it's something I have so much respect for, maybe because it's not my strong suit at all, but it's this decision I think can only come out of love. What a hard lesson to learn over and over! If there's early on in the piece this sort of frontal gaze and the movement of the body is yanking the head along, what's it like, engaging with this notion of what patience is, to also shift your awareness to the kind you have when you're listening and not just trying to make something happen. It's a really different quality. It's not like you're ever really going to have the answers, but I thought maybe I'd figure out a little more. Part of the thing is just "Gosh, I don't know how to fix this and I can try and try and I can try to shift this awareness to this place of humility. I'm not going to push my agenda, but it's so delicate because I think we also live in a world that tells us to be passive, not think and just kind of…fuck it. So when I think about patience, I think about it as a moment by moment yielding, not an easy float down river, and how much that enters the piece, I don't know. But that's been an important guiding idea for some of the material that … if the world establishes this constant undertow, what the audience will see, again ideally, is a sort of reflection of themselves or something they can relate to, but also individual human beings that are struggling to defy that relentless forward motion or to sort of, with humility, try something different. I guess it's this opacity thing that, in certain moments, the humanity of the individual performer would sort of crystallize, even if a moment later they're pulled back into the world. One other thing to say: these kinds of dynamics are things I've worked with in past pieces, but in this one, I didn't want there to be some big showdown of opposites. Even that to me seems too clear cut, for this moment you sort of make these little gains then you're pulled back into it. I wanted it to feel more a lost then found quality, with the piece as a whole might feel more like a loop in the end. I mean, it's not a loop, but as opposed to "we have a trajectory and we've moved from here to there." And I hope that wouldn't come across as a super-dark, negative, hopeless read on it. You know, whenever there's a big revolutionary artistic moment, whether it's in Hip Hop or something like that, how more and more quickly that's co-opted by the market and sold — we're at a point where that turnaround time is so fast that maybe the 60's were like the last time where it could come out and be like "dum-dah-dum!" And maybe that's fitting for that time period, but for this time period it's so…gains are made and then taken into the whole. So that's what I really wanted, that emergence and absorption of the individual humanness, it's not like it comes out and it's clear and we leave the show

feeling …

… feeling whatever programmed emotion you're
supposed to have.

> I want it to feel very slippery, very slippery. And
> that's actually one of the hard things because
> it requires a real finesse on the part of the per-
> formers, and this is what we're waiting to see. My
> real hope is that those moments will come out
> and that, whatever kinds of nerves happen when
> the audience is there, my hope is that it doesn't
> become rigid, because all this subtle emergence
> thing requires a kind of porousness on the part of
> the performers … and that's asking a lot.

＃ *Precious Jennings*[28]

When did you move to Chicago and what brought you here? Had you always grown up dancing, is this something that was always your goal?

Yeah, I grew up dancing. I went to school and did dance class every day. The last 2–3 years of high school was dance every night and on weekends I did competition stuff. I was born in Des Moines, Iowa with my twin sister where I lived until February 2001, when I moved to Chicago with two friends in musical theater, two young men who I was with in a show in Des Moines. There were open classes happening all over the city and I went to every open studio that I could find, and went to these open community classes that Columbia had open, and I started going to classes at Hamlin [Park Theater] even before I started dancing with Chicago Moving Company. I didn't have any

28   Originally published at *Occasional Inquiries*, April. 2, 2016, https://medium.com/occasional-inquiries/in-depth-precious-jennings-relationships-in-idealized-evolution-3596b4fc20b7.

money for school, couldn't afford a plane ticket, or to go to college in Iowa and I was just waiting tables there, so I moved here because I could do the same thing here and have access to all that stuff. There were no dance classes in Des Moines besides the opera gig that I did — because the ballet company that I was with — I was really into ballet when I moved here — that ballet company went defunct in like '98 or '99, so it was just kind of building.

So you were drawn by the culture and to learn more about the art you were interested in.

Yes. I met one of my best friends, Brian Robert-Hinckle, we were in a circus together, and we ended up living in the same area together. I was in Rogers Park and he was off of Granville, and we did this circus in Aurora, the Walter Peyton Roundhouse, and we got paid this great chunk of money every weekend for like 4 or 5 months, we got paid rehearsals and we became tight friends. He was in school at Columbia and he introduced me to all these people and we have always worked together and still make work with the group I'm in with Rachel Bunting, The Humans. He was going to be a part of this but the scheduling didn't work. And that's how it evolved, just through creating relationships with people; I moved here knowing no one. The two people I moved here with ended up moving away.

That must have been isolating.

> It was and it wasn't. They went to go do Summer-stock and they ended up not coming back, and I was just like "Oh, all right." It was before 9/11, so there were jobs and I ended up getting hired on part time, doing temp work, and I had a job within 4 months, a solid job, so I didn't have to temp anymore. I waited tables for about 6 months then quit that, but they let me come and go as I wanted, so I'd go take class in the morning, come in the afternoon, stay 'til 7, go to class, come back.

How did you come up with the idea for the program
you're working on now?

> I'd been a part of other people's processes from beginning to end in supporting their research, being a large part of their research and I did a piece I think in 2007 combining voice and move-ment, part of the Field Works at the old Links Hall. That was my first solo thing, looking at sound, movement and improvisation —

That's interesting, there's this shift that happened
for you, somewhere in all of this, between ballet and
improvisation?

> Yes. There was this huge shift. In 2002, Brian Rob-ert-Hinckle and I went to this festival — I mean, growing up, I did ballet, jazz, I had this dream of

one day doing Stomp — I was a percussionist also, so that translated for me — in 2002 we went to Bates, where I did this body percussion class, and another, body harmonics, where every afternoon we did mind-body centering and then into Thai massage — so looking at the energetic body and the cellular body. growing up, I was always into science too, and always thought there was something else going on. Yes, ballet is great, movement is great but someone taught me meditation when I was growing up, and every night I would meditate and think to myself, "There's something else going on." Whatever that means. So, at the Bates Dance Festival I got more into this whole other world of movement that's possible in improvisation.

How would you categorize it? As a kind of spirituality or as a kind of visualization technique?

I think it was very grounding for me, and I was this person in space — spiritual? I don't know. Maybe. I know my spirit changed, there was something that I wasn't going to let go of easily. Maybe that has to do with spirit? I think improvisation came in early on — I remember one specific day growing up where my dance teacher said to me, "Oh, you can come and practice." And I remember thinking, "Okay, what the hell do I do standing here all by myself?" and just playing around with really simple things, and then realized, "Oh! I can create something by myself," and I think I came back to that at Bates and I worked with a Japanese choreographer there where the energy really became solidified and the performance of emotions — because growing up, I didn't really like the competition part because it was all so much fake and contrived emotions people were conveying. It wasn't at the level it is now in performance, but this Japanese choreographer was so slow in building up, from the inside, and he would give a direction and say, "No, that's not you." So I began asking, where does the performance come from, I think, which was improvisation.

Who was the choreographer?

He was actually an engineer, he wasn't a performer. He built robotics, Fukurow Ishikawa. And then there was another, Kosei Sakamoto was the artist in residence there at the time — two Japanese men — so Bates was a really big shift. Then I came back here, did the massage studies, did yoga — that was my first big experience with a yoga class every day for 3 weeks. I drove a car there and I couldn't actually lay down all the way, extend my right leg, for the entire time there — I think it was from having to press down and hold the gas pedal driving that distance from here to there, or maybe an injury to my foot from the year before. So then I came back here, met a bunch of teachers including — Kathleen Hermesdorf was at Bates that year and we all went and did a workshop with her in San Francisco in 2003. She talked a lot about energy and was working with the elements and dance in creating improvisation — and then I came back here and thought, "I want to know more about this." And that's present in the work I do now, it definitely is; I went to the Pacific College of Oriental Medicine and learned about Chinese Theory and Chi Gong, which Kathleen usually incorporates. Then I met Rachel Bunting and she introduced me to teaching actors by having me come teach anatomy to her class and then I said "Whoa, this is really great, they're so unlike dancers and I can really use what I know in a really simple way to get people into thinking about how they move, people who don't move. So then I met [former Chicago Moving Company Artistic Director Elizabeth] "Nana" Shineflug, and we had a lot of similar ways of moving and she went, "Okay, come take classes with me," and then I met K.J. Holmes in 2007. In those intervening years, I performed a lot, did a lot of DIY stuff, and then started a duet with Rachel that we did a few years, with multiple years of research work in-between with lots of works-in-progress performances. Specific to improvisation aside from that, Ayako Kato and I would do short improvisations and research, I would do yearly workshops with K.J., I think I missed a year in '09 or '10; I'd go to Movement Research or she'd come here. And the last 3 years I've been at Bearnstow in Mt. Vernon, Maine, which is where most of the research for this has taken place.

In 2011, someone gave me a bunch of these cassette tapes — actually Daniel Guidara, the Tai-chi teacher at Hamlin Park. I got a car and it had a tape player, and he was all, "Ahh! I have a bunch of tapes for you." So he gave me all these tapes and I picked one up and it was *Whale Nation.* I was like, "Hmm!" I was driving home to Iowa, and I put it in, and I was like, "Whoaaaa! Amazing!" I listened to it for probably 2 months straight, that was all that was in my car. If anyone got in, I was like, "Ummm, I've been listening to a book on tape." Anyway, it's really amazing, it talks about whales — I think it was made in 1987 or something — Heathcoat Williams is the publisher (editor's note: Heathcoat is actually the poet-author of the book); I'm not sure if it's a book or it may just have been a book on tape. So, that was a huge thing. Then my friend Jeff Giza and I were going to do this improvisation that was in this attic in Pilsen, just go and he was going to play drums and I was going to dance, cool, awesome and then, the day of the performance, he says "Oh my God, I can't get into my space to get my drums." I was like, "Okay, we're performing tonight." Here's the practice of improvisation: I was like "Okay, don't worry about it." And he was like, "But I still want to come and watch you." And I was like, "Don't worry about it!" And…I had an idea! So…I went and taught my yoga class in the morning and was all, "Okay, okay, okay." And, for some reason, while I was home with my dad, I asked him, "Can you put this on digital in case something happens to it?" So then I had a digital copy of the file, and I blew it into iTunes, spliced it out, frantically ran around my apartment and just grabbed stuff…I mean not frantically, very mindfully. Ha! I just ran around, grabbed these objects, set up the space, and edited these little objects within the hour, I mean, it was like 15 minutes from within the hour of book on tape, and did a performance. Maybe a 15…18, 20 minute performance?

So this recording is someone talking about whales.

No, right. It's about the history of whales and the industrialization of the world, built on the back of whales and the world, beauty products and —

Lamp oil…

— lamp oil, and the astronauts going into space, all of the moving parts that come from the sperm whale oil; medicines and most every major city made for import/export were built for whaling communities…so, islands, all this history is huge. So that was inspiring in many ways, and that was in 2012 and I let it lay, went and worked on other people's work, but still listened to my book on tape on whales, and would get all hooked in and be like, "Oh, what does that really mean? How the world is now?"

So were you thinking about that, about the history
of industrialization as you started to move toward
making this piece?

> I don't even know what that means, how to think
> about industrialization in terms of how you build
> a structure in improvisation, and the relationship
> between everybody in the space and how the whale
> moves through the oceans and there's this whole
> other thing they don't know about that's affect-
> ing how they migrate or…now, I've watched every
> documentary there is on whales…and there's a
> new one, because all the fish are being wiped out
> over here and shifting the ecosystem of the ocean,
> then the whales don't have anything to feed on and
> then they have to go migrate to go and find food,
> so there's that large-scale shift.

It sounds like you basically became a marine
zoologist.

> I don't know…ha! Yeah, and working with musi-
> cians, and writers and water is the holders of
> emotions…so, while I was working with K.J. at
> Bearnstow, the first year I went there, she was
> like, "Just bring a seed," and I was like, "I've got
> whales and I've been reading this," and there's a
> huge lake that most often in the morning, but
> usually 3 times a day, we would go get in the lake.
> After class, wander down, get in the lake. And it's
> a glacial lake, so it's colder. I did a lot of processing

from my personal life there, I did a lot of writing and singing and walking in the forest and it was this huge, enchanted, magical thing. And then I did a solo. I was processing relationships, it was in 2012, I think I had come then from doing a lot of performance and teaching and that was my time to actual unpack, away from all that, time you don't have for yourself. Yeah, unpack, relationships, getting to know myself again, being outside of relationships, or in relationships, or being around people that I know. And working with some of the people I do for so many years, I mean, I work with my best friend. What do I want to do with that outside of supporting another person's work, what are my interests? I need to take a little time for that. And then, if I do that, then I can do this other thing, or this, and I was working with Ayako a lot for the piece I did for that.

It sounds like maybe you were going through some relationship difficulties at the time.

Yeah. Nothing I want to talk about. Positive, I mean. I find all relationships positive, whether they're negative at the time or not, ha ha! But yeah, I have a lot of writing from then that I go back to, but that's part of the work also is me, it's part of this — which I talk about a lot — it's taking something really, really personal and how do you go into it, looking at performance — I talk about this with my students all the time that there is that

— eww, it's not ready to show yet, it's something for you and not something that's ready to show yet, the personal has to expand out into the universal.

Right. So you're combining a lot of things. Symbology, such as with the water of the subconscious you referenced earlier, this zoology —

Yes, and the developmental movement patterns, I was looking at that, from Body-Mind centering, thinking about the body from it in utero stages, of humans, how we start out suspended in water with no sense of time and space, we don't sense gravity; we sense gravity through another person's body. And through another person's sense of gravity that's carrying you through space and then, looking at that in different ways and looking at the development of the chakra system and development of that into emotions and energy, and layering that through — as we sense gravity, the two main chakras that are open when we're born is the root which deals with earth and the crown which deals with — I mean, I babies have a different sense of connection that builds through the spine — so then, as we start to come into relationship with gravity, we start to build up to standing, and the chakras do the same thing. It's in that first 7 years — we develop our bodies at the same time we develop relationship and emotion and how we perceive ourselves in the world. As we develop and find our movement patterns, how we either relate to space or people, how we were treated once we're born, the environment we develop in constitutes how the chakras are formed.

And there's an order to that that determines the movement?

Yes. Well, it's the chicken or the egg. If someone's screaming at you, you're either going to scream and yell at the back or retreat and just implode in on yourself, which then automatically affects your movement patterning. You can get into the psychotherapy and all of that but I'm more interested in experiencing it, really getting into all of that but having a place of play. So that's sort of my focus, not getting into the specifics of balance and imbalance, but being able to play with that. Not even thinking about the chakras, but going into movement, developmental movement and improvising with that jumping-off point and then, the Bonnie Bainbridge Cohen — that's who K.J.'s teacher was — her Body-Mind Centering separates the physical body into different parts, so I've been combining the BMC work into the chakra work. So I've got this and then I've got the horse, so I feel like what I'm doing now is the groundwork into "How do I relay all this information to people, and then how do I create with it?" So it's about having specificity which, working with horses you need to have extreme specificity...

Can you explain a little for readers how the horse
aspect of this production comes into play?

> So, I'm looking at two different nervous systems.
> Whales have this bigger emotional center, the
> hypothalamus, so looking at this holder of emo-
> tion, in this huge animal, floating in water, they
> live in pods — a.k.a. herds — I've been relating
> that to the organ systems and fat and floating, and
> then looking at the horse's nervous systems, these
> sort of super-anxious, high-tone and, since they're
> a prey animal, they're usually on-guard and very
> sensitive. I did that research with Rachel [Bun-
> ting], so that's where that aspect of the research
> comes from too, I guess. I was really enamoured
> — my brother-in-law's father, he bred horses
> — he has one horse now, he kind of sold them.
> But I would go there, I went there a few times
> and he has mares, which are supposed to live in a
> herd — there's a place in Michigan where they let
> them live in a herd, but they're still captive — so
> I would watch the mares and their foals. An even
> just being invited in, at one time I think he had
> six mares and their babies, which is kind of a lot.
> And the moms will get super pushy with you if
> they don't want you near, so like looking at how
> they care about their young.

Why did you want to move from just looking at the
whales?

Oh! That was from at Bearnstow also, the stuff that I did with Rachel was there. And the place I went in Michigan, I went there for a leadership conference on mindful practices, all the admin team I was with went to this horse place and did this leadership course. In it, we had all these tasks to do, we met the herd, went up to pet them and blah blah blah and then they were like, "Okay, in groups of 5, you can't touch the horse, but you have to go and try and get it to come from the back to the front of the field and go through this obstacle field, and they would take away, "Okay, you can't touch. Okay, now you can touch. Now you can't use the begging, pretend you're giving them a treat. You can't use sound or yell or talk to the horse. So it was about a half hour, so we had to call upon rhythm and moving and getting close to the horse and moving, then going far away. It was almost impossible. Most everybody got their horse up but then they were totally not interested and totally just wanted to eat the grass. And then we all sit in a circle and talk about it — it's a husband and wife that own the place — and then literally not 3 minutes into talking the horses come in, stick their head in like, "Hey guys, how you doing?" It was amazing, they're totally social animals, they want relationships but if the relationship isn't more interesting than what they're eating, or if it's just what they want to do because they eat lots of food, they're very big animals, then they're not going to be engaged. So, it's like what do you have to offer them? It's a trust issue. So the horse ideas came into my work at Bearnstow in 2014 and I stayed for a week after just to work on stuff and they have 2 horses there and I would take them for walks to get grass. A quarter mile up the road, there was a field of clovers they liked and I would walk up there with them and build trust and, at first, he wouldn't walk with me. Then, one day, he started to push me off the road and I was like, "Seriously, he's going to push me into the ditch." So I'd push him back and he was like, "Hm. Okay." So we'd walk and he'd get closer and closer and he would come up to me and say hello for a little bit, or he would push the other horse and they'd have this little archetypal relationship. He'd push the other horse to me, and be like "You. You go play with her," and he was the alpha. So that sort of spurred my relationship with the horses. And now I'm here.

Right! And so, in that confluence of research and investigation into different systems, where do you feel as though the project is now?

Now it's in this place where I'm trying to make work that's accessible and non-judgmental and not just for dancers, looking at the relationship of everyone who is creating the world of this performance and not only just the performers, there's this whole thing out here called an audience that you're asking to engage with you. Because that's

what performance is, which is like how you get
a horse to be interested in you; and also, it's just
like letting go of that and really honing into the
relationship, especially with improvisation. You
aren't just playing to the audience, at the same time
you have to create in-depth relationships with the
musicians, with whoever else may be in the space.
I'm working with people I've never worked with
before, or whom I even knew before this, which
is what I knew going into this residency when I
called all my old friends and they were like, "No,
it doesn't work with my schedule." And another
thing had spurred this was doing the Three on
Three program here a few years ago, and that was
with a close group of friends that I'd been per-
forming with a few years, and two musicians. And
I was giving them very little to go on, just "stay
in solo and see what happens," and then another
friend was projecting images and I got pulled in
and thought, "I want to look into this." I was sort
of going off the work with horses then.

How do you see all this coming together?

We're setting up a working body and working
mind. The performance comes in the practice, so
what you're seeing is a polished practice. Hopefully
the audience, like my performers, will learn more
about themselves, looking at the capacity we have
to be in a relationship to each other, the world, to
the group and no one way of sensing it is right or

wrong — and to have fun. That's been my motto for the residency, is to play. Everything is in play, and I want the audience to experience that joy, or sadness, or fright. That's what we're getting into now, finding this place of earth together. We've chosen one chakra to be together in and then everybody else is choosing another personal chakra to work within. You can kind of stereotype each chakra — the heart has to do with compassion, for instance, and then you get into how would you describe that in theater and acting terms, that would be: "I take care of myself and that's the only person I'm concerned with," or: "Oh, let me take care of you, can I help you?" So, playing with that. Am I directing people within that? No, they're doing it themselves. I'm giving them a means and a structure to do it within. I'll lead them through something and it can be different everyday — their emotional and personal lives change every day so we always come into the room with a new mind and body — but it's also this question of can they drop into a specific place, which I am asking them to do. I am asking them to choose a specific place to work within, and then you can toy with it. It can be sort of like a melting pot where nobody knows what to do, so they all roll around on the floor ha haaaa! Unless that's it, and it can totally happen unless it has meaning, and sometimes you unpack shit you didn't know you had; we're creating this work in this space, and I know we're going to look at it in a completely different way.

Pidgeon Pagonis [29]

Why this fear of intersexuality?

I think of intersex, non-binary or trans people — I'm not saying these were the names given throughout time — but people of intermediate sex and gender throughout history have actually, for the majority of history, been revered and been given special roles in culture and in society. So I think the fear we see today, or what appears as a fear or at least a violence toward our bodies is a very recent invention that started around the medieval era when Christianity was used in a way that I don't think it was supposed to be, that the Bible was used in a way that's not what the Bible states, but they've used it in a way to state that anything that's intermediate in terms of sex or gender

29 Originally published in *Newcity, April 26, 2017, https://newcity.com/2017/05/04/pidgeon-pagonis-and-the-fight-for-intersex-rights*. As written by *Newcity* editors, this colophon was added: "*Post-publication, Pagonis asks that readers note that, in the section "why the fear of intersexuality" many of the ideas and concepts they shared in that section they learned from their colleague Cary Gabriel Costello who gave a talk that they attended right before the interview, and many of the ideas he shared in that talk were fresh in their mind.*"

is an abomination against God or unnatural and you see at the same time a witch hunt, literally for all types of people: for witches, for Muslims, for Jews and at the same time you see people who existed freely before this time or were seen as better than other people, you see their bodies being attacked in ways that you would see other people being attacked who weren't Christians. So I think it's important to keep in mind that this is a very recent thing and the medicalization aspect is even more recent, it's only been since the 1940s onward that our bodies have been altered by medical professionals. I think you see at the same time in the early 1900s a standardization process happening across the board in capitalism. You see railroad tracks being standardized — the widths of them — and you see the medical profession making an effort to standardize care and standardize bodies and things like that and, at the same time, intersex bodies with intersex genitals get standardized and put into one or the other categories. So I think intersex people are a manifestation of the history of going at anybody who isn't considered normal — I guess it is fear because there's a threat of power and a threat that the power will be taken away from the people in power and I think that the core of it is that intersex shakes the core of this idea that there are two sexes and two genders and one side — the male side — is above the female side and there's a power dynamic there and I think intersexuality shakes that myth at its core. So I think we get pushed back into one or the other — actually, we get pushed back into the female role because as John Money, the doctor, is famous for saying, "It's easier to dig a hole than build a pole." I think there's a fear and a history of this othering and scapegoating people seen as others whom are really seen as a threat to a lot of things really, like a certain religion or economies of capitalism or governments and societies — so yes. I think there are people who take Christianity and use it in the wrong way that it was not meant to and I think that speaks to how in medicine it clouds their vision of how they see difference in the same way.

Your struggle with this still-pervasive policy of non-consensual medical interventions reminds me of the problems the medical industry faced in the slow acceptance for the movement for hospice care, or in having to face its problems with drug lobbying, especially during the AIDS crisis. Do you see attitudes changing?

I was speaking Monday at Rush Medical University and some of the feedback we heard was that I was part of the problem that until this point I didn't understand this is what they had to do with intersex people and now they completely feel different. So I definitely think there's a group of people growing up today whom are going to be medical professionals or already are who are definitely changing and that's awesome, and that's beautiful. And then I think there are people already in these roles, the pediatric urologists especially whom are very entrenched in their ways but I don't think it's ever too late for somebody to change their ideas or attitudes. I think some people refuse to do so because they definitely have an idea of who they are and nobody wants to think they're doing harm to people, that's just not good for anybody's psyche. So, I think those people who are a little more reticent to change, it's a struggle with them and they don't want to think of themselves causing harm to people. But I do see change happening and I am confident and I'm one-hundred-percent certain that we're going to see a reversal of how intersex people are treated as kids in this world very, very soon. Within my lifetime.

You were born with an endocrinological condition described as "androgen insensitivity syndrome" for which, as a child, doctors performed surgery on you. What have been the results of that for you personally?

I think you get this and know this, but I just want to say it [for readers] that I believe I was born with an intersex variation and intersex sex traits and I don't believe I have a syndrome or a disorder and I think it's unfortunate that that's the language that gets used for that even by well-meaning doctors or academics because if you read it and just gloss it over, you think "Oh, this person has a disorder or a syndrome or a condition and so they got help," and then everyone just sort of goes on with their life. But I think when we start to understand sex as not just a binary — and gender as well — then we start to get to see that these treatments are ridiculous and purely cosmetic most of the time. So anyways, because I was born that way, they did three things: they removed my internal gonads, they removed my clitoris and then they did a vagioplasty and they put me on a lot of hormones, on hormone therapy. So the results of these interventions, well, the first result, was that I grew up thinking that there was something wrong with me, that I had cancer — they lied to me and told me that I had cancer in my ovaries when I was born and that's why they had to remove them. That's what they told a lot of us with intersex variation. They have to explain the scar so they say, "Oh, it was cancer and we took out your ovaries." [laughs] So that was scary growing up, thinking I had cancer and that it might return one day. And also, the other things they did, always putting your body on display — I'd have to go to the doctor and pull down my pants and lift up my shirt and they look at you and touch you and I think I learned quickly that I didn't own my body, that other people had access to it and it brought a lot of shame about my body because I just felt there must be something to be ashamed about if I have to continually go to the doctor and I was told not to tell anybody, not even people I was dating or my best friends because they said rumors could start going around and the only people I needed to share anything with — and what they all ignored at that time was that I couldn't have children because I didn't have ovaries because I'd had cancer, quote unquote. So I think that was one of the longest-lasting effects was this sense of your body's not yours and that you should be ashamed of your body and yourself. Then, the third — which is more of a physical effect — is the lack of sensation, sensitivity, etcetera and the pain that is actually a remnant of the surgeries and the scar tissue and the nerve damage that had been caused by the surgeries. It just sucks.

I know you see how important it is to speak out about this problem in the medical community — is that what motivated you to testify for the Inter-American Commission on Human Rights? What do you think have been the outcomes to your testimony there?

Nothing, really. I think it has led to a little more of an increased interest. I think they just held a bunch of hearings recently — I believe the same type of hearing, the same type of people — I think it has put things on the books, set things in motion. I think it's better than nothing. I think we're going to start seeing those outcomes with the case in South Carolina, #justice4mc [filed in support of a minor subjected to surgical intervention] actually.

If that comes out in our favor, then that could set a precedent with the doctors in this country so they could see that there are indeed legal ramifications if they continue in what they're doing. The U.N. recently has come out and said that these are human rights violations, the medical protocols that are happening to us and that was really important on paper too, but the US has a long history of ignoring the U.N., especially when it comes to the rights of children — or the rights of women, or the rights of people who are not white, straight, cis men. So I think everybody plays a really valid role in activism and people whom put energy into these departments, it's all part of the puzzle. But I think for me, personally, I've gotten to the breaking point where I'm like, "We need to start doing in-person actions at the hospitals." I want to focus that in Chicago visibly on Lurie [Children's Hospital], so they become the very first hospital to say "Hey, this is wrong, we've learned from our mistakes of the past and we want to move forward working with the intersex community, respecting their wishes instead of going against them, and I think we have some ins with them because I think they're trying to be better" and I think I can be like, "This is how you can be better."

You performed in the last season of *Transparent*. Why was this important to you and what do you think the outcome of that experience was?

A lot of intersex people talk about how there's no real representation of us in media and when there is, we're usually characterized in a negative or freakish light, as someone who's got a weird medical condition. And I think it was a positive instance of representation, which was really cool, in a show that's doing really groundbreaking work in the trans media and so, when I was asked to do this, I was like, "Okay." I would take almost any opportunity to give positive representation of intersex people in any way that I can. I don't know if there was any real outcome to that, but I can imagine it created a little more notoriety for intersex people in the lives of people who watch the show and are tuned into trans issues already, and then they heard "intersex," and learned a little more about it.

So given all this, as someone who's so engaged as an activist for intersexuality, what do you see as some of the biggest challenges for society and the intersex community on the ground today?

I think the biggest challenge is the way our society is currently set up to look for gratification or love for purpose to being here as humans, we look for that externally to ourselves, whether it's a purchase of goods or whatever instead of looking for that inwardly. So I think that when doctors see our bodies with an intermediate sex they think we could never find love or purpose without looking "normal," and that they think they can bring his external process to our bodies through plastic surgery and give us our happiness through that. I think we have to first rid society of this idea that you're not good enough as you are, and you must have X-Y and Z to be valid in this society, whether it's a car or a job or look a certain way or whatever and how do we look and find that for ourselves internally and push that. I think something really positive happened when I spoke with this pediatric urologist at Lurie, and I said to him, "I think you really need to love yourself before you can love others and I think you need to take care of yourself before you can take care of others," and he literally laughed and almost choked on his laughter and was like, "I don't love myself — I love my wife, I love my kids, but I don't love my *self*," and I think that's a big thing because I really think they believe they're helping us. And as long as we live in a society where that's how you find certain, external gratification, then we're going to keep running into these walls with intersex communities.

John Waters [30]

Your commencement speech you gave at the Rhode Island School of Design about pushing boundaries went viral on the internet. It's all about the possibility of pushing back against bigotry — against class, race, sex and all of it — as a reason to become an artist. The subversiveness of art as a means for good. Why do you think it went viral in a world where individual self-interest seems to be such an insurmountable force, especially lately in our politics?

> I think it went viral because mostly, graduation speeches — and to be honest, I had never seen any because I had never read one for anyone — I'd never been somewhere where there was a commencement speech, even my own. So I think I was earnest in my advice, I did give good advice but I think I gave alternative advice and I was mindful — my target was the problem graduate, someone whom might have taken 8 years to get

through college or had to commit a robbery to get their tuition. And I also talked to the parents about what brats the kids could be and I think the parents really responded well to that because people don't usually address the other side of the issue.

Thinking of this whole thing about viral memes — I was curious if this is something you yourself even put out there — as a writer, the whole "don't (have sex with) people who don't read" meme was another favorite of mine.

Yeah, somebody did that to cute it up. But certainly — yes, I think if you go in someone's house and they don't have one thing to read — although there's also the opposite of that: if they have stuff to read in the bathroom, I don't think you should have sex with them either.

Make Trouble, as I was reading it, tracked a little for me like a children's book for adults —

Damaged children!

None other. But speaking of, it got me thinking about this camp sleepaway you're now doing for grown-ups. I've been seeing that out there a lot lately.

Yeah, that's a whole other thing though that I promised to another exclusive and blah blah blah. It just goes with all this personal tour stuff I'm doing — I have this spoken word show I do two versions of — many versions, actually. I have one called "This Filthy World" that I do all year, I have a Christmas show that's already booked this year again that's 18 cities in 20 days. I have a horror festival version, I have a gay version — I know that sounds redundant — I have a prison version, I have a version that I've done at rock festivals; so I make a great part of my living by traveling and speaking. To me, it's like being a politician, you meet your audience, you constantly see the people and they're getting younger for me which is really, really encouraging. I get older and my audience gets younger. It couldn't be better. I mean, last night we had a signing at Book Soup in LA and we sold almost 400 books — that's pretty good — and the greatest thing is that all my fans get their roots done for me. I really think beauticians should be happy about me visiting because whenever I come to town, everyone's roots are freshly done!

And so, about the book, how did you meet Eric Hanson who did the illustrations that are such a big part of it?

I met him because he did the cover of *Role Models* and I absolutely loved the cover. I'd never met him but he did the cover and I loved it so much, so that's why I wanted him to do this because I knew he knew how to be poetically elegant.

Speaking of *Role Models*, and all the classism and racism built into our prison-industrial system, your visits to prisons for that book read as a sort of art as activism, too. Radical empathy. Do you think art can actually change things? There's a lot of conversation out there about using art as a resistance, do you think it's possible for art to have an effect on situations like the problems we have with mass incarceration?

> Yeah, I mean the biggest activism out there right now is *Saturday Night Live*. Nothing is more effective than that right now in terms of reaching a wide audience to make fun of Trump. It's incredibly brilliant activism, I think and I'm for that, it's using humor again as terrorism like the Yippies did, to make fun of the enemy until they squirm in embarrassment and that's fair, that's good terrorism to me. You have to make each other laugh. If you just go out there and are preaching, no one's going to listen. You know, I'm not a separatist, I'm friends with some people who voted for Trump, not many. Nobody has the nerve to tell me, but a few have.

I'm always intrigued by this question about whether it's effective, or if it's just entertainment, like taking selfies. Does it change anything?

> Taking selfies: I don't do it, but obviously the whole world does it. So even when I'm on these books tours and you offer to take a picture

together, then they don't want to do a selfie. So, the selfie has become — it takes twice as long to do as an autograph. I do it because I'm like, "What am I going to do, these people bought me my house." Why am I not going to take a picture with them except I always say, "You have to hold it up! Shoot down or it's really ugly if you shoot up!" So not only does it take longer, you have to teach them camera angles.

Young people, who embraced the selfie — so, in meeting so many young people, do you find they're receptive to the ideas in it?

My audience, they're already so receptive to it, they're actually buying it to give to other people they want to be role models for, people in their family. I mean — who'd have thought I'd ever be a gift item. But still, I think it is a good one for a certain type of graduate.

Right, and the role models from your visits in prison, have you kept in touch with some of those who may have graduated back out into the world?

Yes, and some of those I helped get out are doing very, very well. And I do have a couple of friends still in prison whom I do visit. I think it's important to visit people in prison. And if you know anyone in prison, I would encourage you very much to visit them. They're a good audience! I

always get good letters from prisoners. I don't usu-
ally answer them because I have a lot going on in
my life, but I get some really good ones, I get some
really good letters from prison.

I think about art that way as doing something, and
about Johnny Cash visiting Folsom, about how
important that is for artists to empathize with people
even in the face of their exploitation by society.

And books — books are the most important thing
in prison, it's the only way you can escape it.

Jacinda Ratcliffe[31]

You're originally from Virginia, correct?

I came up here to double major in dance and psychology at Northwestern. Up to that point, I had just done ballet and tap and that was kind of my thing. I stopped tapping in college but continued in ballet. It was a Modern based program, though and so going from that extreme to the other opened myself up to the possibilities for this whole other side of dance, and that being a ballerina isn't particularly satisfying. You don't know that as a 17 year old. So, experienced that, did some summer intensive and I remember I went to the San Francisco Conservatory of Dance after my junior year in college and that was my first time doing contemporary. You start the day with ballet and then use the technique to do *not* ballet and it was like 9 to 6 or 10 to 6 every day and that was when I was like, "This is actually what I want

31   Originally published at *Art Intercepts*, Nov. 16, 2017, http://www.artintercepts. org/2017/11/16/movement-matters-an-interview-with-jacinda-ratcliffe.

to be doing." So, post-grad, I remember it was February and I was like, "I have no plans!" But I wanted to stay in Chicago because the Northwestern program, all the professors very much work in Chicago and it kind of feeds you into this scene and I started researching the audition program at Lou Conte, went in and got in and that first summer I was still living in Evanston and just couldn't find a job. I just wanted to find a service industry job, bartending and just could not find it in the summer and so all I had to do every day that summer was just show up and take classes. It was hard, it's all advanced pro-classes and in the summer time everybody's off-contract and taking classes. Amazing professionals, they all worked so hard going in and taking classes in the evening and in that time I felt like I grew a lot. Then I stayed for the yearlong program and that's when I started freelance working in Chicago, ended up getting a second scholarship and continued working and then in June decided the next step for me is moving to New York. So that's happening.

Who were you dancing for/with in San Francisco?

Alex Ketley's work was something that we studied a lot, even though I didn't get to actually study with him. We also learned a Robert Moses piece and got to work with Christian Burns piecing together different things. But one of the things, if I can relate my study of psychology to it: Summerly

> Ratigan runs the school and so she danced with lines for a very long time and talked to us a lot about letting go. And letting go in the need to know. She was like, "Every day I'm going to show up from 9 to 6 and I'm going to be dancing. And that's all I need to know." So schedule is posted daily which is like, most intensives, they send you the whole schedule right away and you're like, "Okay, Tuesday is the 3rd week I'm taking partnering," but why do you need to know that weeks in advance? I know my first class is going to start at 9:30, and I'm going to be there all day.

What compelled you to pair up these two different fields of study?

> Psychology's always been something that interests me. Knowing the stigma around it and feeling like we just don't give enough credit to taking care of our minds. Even something as simple as theoretically once a year going in and you get a physical checkup and twice a year you go to the dentist, my eyes. We check in with everything else but the simple act of going in to see a psychologist just to chat about your own mental health. It's so hard when it doesn't have physical symptoms. You know, I've had my own struggles with it and in high school it was something that interested me. I've always been good at talking to people.

Do you think about it through the lens, for instance, of dance?

I don't think about it in terms of dance therapy specifically, but in more how taking care of your mental health allows for dance to be more ... especially in the ballet world — if I can make a blanket statement, whatever everyone has their own struggles — but it can be very taxing on the mind. We're staring at ourselves in mirrors for hours on end every single day and night. It's unhealthy. And it's always like, "Oh, I need to improve, I can do better at this, I'm not strong enough here."

Right. This constant struggle to have the right sort of body image, to stay below a certain perceived acceptable weight, that sort of thing.

And always working on technique, "Oh my turn out isn't where it should be," or "I can't get on my legs so I'm falling out of all my pirouettes today." Sort of learning how to manage those thoughts and give yourself tools to in the moment be like, "I fell out of a turn, but that doesn't make me a bad dancer."

Right, that it's just trial and error. Practice, and psychological elasticity.

And I feel like it's a tool we all constantly have to work at. I very much think about psychology as a tool that can make us better dancers. It's just not something I think we talk about enough.

Were your parents encouraging you to study these
subjects? Is it something that they were doing for
work?

> No, when we were little, my parents just put us in
> everything. I played soccer for a very long time,
> I played basketball, dance. I was into everything.
> It's like a running joke in my family, my dad, that
> no one knows what he does. He works the 9-5 in
> like risk management. His last job title was like 8
> words long. I remember take your kids to work day
> every year he'd have the wipe board and sketch out
> like this happens, then this happens and then the
> banks. He used to work for like Freddie Mac in
> mortgages, back before the government took over.
> Then, my mom would do a lot of management
> type stuff but then just a year ago graduated with
> her Bachelor's. She immigrated from the Congo
> when she was 19, and went to high school not
> knowing English very well and graduated into
> the work force, she had got her Associate's but
> then while I was in college decided she needed
> to finish so graduated with a degree in HR. They
> were both athletes, though. My dad very much
> treats me like his athlete child, like, "Are you get-
> ting your protein? How are your injuries?" They're
> really supportive. I feel lucky in that sense.

It's interesting too, how powerful that encouragement
must have been, since when you started the represen-
tation of people of color in dance was a real problem.

Yes, there have been real strides in recent years. Misty Copeland, and that sort of thing. When I was little, I remember being in the Nutcracker and they were like, "Your hair has to be curled for the party scene." And I was like, "Oh, I have curly hair, I'm set." Then my teacher literally said to me the words, "People didn't have hair like you back then. You have to straighten it then curl it so you fit into what the aesthetic is." At the time, I'm 12, 13 years old and it doesn't even occur to me that that's a thing. I remember my mom getting offended and me being like, no, no, no, it'll just be a few hours and I'll have to deal with changing it but just truly not understanding why that's problematic. You know, you're doing a ballet, and ballet is so obviously not the representation of what was literally happening back then.

Right, but as an art form, people see in it the expression of their own racial, sex and gender ideals and sometimes their own bigotries.

Yes, and gender's a whole other thing, but it's definitely a thing that I've learned to embrace. You know, I used to then go and straighten my hair for every single performance, again, this was all happening so subconsciously that it wasn't until recently, until the latter half of college, where I was like, "I'm okay, I'm okay just being who I am." I do think throughout the history of dance, there have been pieces with people blending together and becoming more representative but it's shocking that it took us until the 21st century to get Misty Copeland. It's kind of like, "Oh, we had a black president, racism is done. Oh Misty Copeland's a principal, so everything is fine now." And even with her, she gets the contemporary stuff and not the classical, that was from her early career. I read her book *The Unlikely Ballerina*, and she talks about doing Swan Lake and you put on the makeup and make yourself the White Swan.

White-facing it.

Right, so people are talking about it a lot more, and if you're not actively fighting it, you're possibly letting it happen.

Bill Ayers

Chicago is the home of this connection between socially-engaged art and social movements and so I wanted to speak with you because I'd read your most recent book, and wanted to discuss those connections between art and activism with you. Part of the fundamental role of the historical avant-garde was pushing back against instrumental rationality and its overreaches, motivated by this bottom-line thinking about everything, which is what neoliberalism has been all about embracing. I think the standard for when I'm reading is that I learn something new, which I think is the same for both the art and the activism I care most about, that they teach me something. One of the things you discuss, for instance, is this push to privatize everything, including the public school systems, and you talk about the Pay for Success program which I was shocked to read about.

> We talk abstractly about privatizing and monetizing everything, but when we get into the weeds around it, almost anything — normal people

> whom don't go into the weeds hear something like "austerity," or "privatizing," and they think, "meh, whatever. It's kind of normal." It's not normal! It's insane and if you look at the details of what they're talking about, it boggles your mind. You can take anything — my granddaughter's been in public school for years and when they outsourced the janitorial services, the school went to filth. It just went, "why not?" because it's like the Flint water crisis. If it's a private matter, if it's not a public need then we're trying to cut staff, cut salaries, do less work, make more profit. So Flint is completely a case study and in a small way it happened at her school. They took away the janitors, you no longer had a custodian whom was responsible for the school, whatever corruption and weirdness might have been involved in that, now you have a situation where a group of outsiders would come in, do a quick job and get out.

Right, it's all bottom-line standards. Part of me is shocked they keep getting these things through.

> I want you to be shocked. Yes; bottom line instead of public interest. So, programs like Pay For Success are just an atrocity. I don't think we should get used to it. You know, you say your standard for reading is, "did I learn something?" Well, my standard for activism is exactly that. When you do an action, when you run a campaign, the question is what did you learn and what did you

teach. Not how did you look on TV and not how did you look with that mask and molotov cocktail in hand, what did you accomplish in terms of your own growth and learning and in terms of what you taught somebody? If you didn't teach and you didn't learn then no matter how you felt about it, it wasn't worthwhile. If you taught some groups of people and learned yourself, then yeah, let's keep going. I think that's really important as a kind of pedagogical standard for activism, for reading. Is it worthwhile. I think that's terribly important. I was in a meeting this weekend and we went around and introduced ourselves and a couple people said "I've been an activist for 40 years," or "I've been an activist for 30 years." I hate hearing that, even though I've been an activist for 40 years, and the reason I hate hearing it is that it has an intent or it has an effect that is, "I know more, you can trust me." And that's not true. For example, one of the most obvious public examples of this is whom owns Martin Luther King? Does John Lewis own Martin Luther King because he was on the bridge with him? Or are the young activists whom are enacting Martin Luther King, do they have a better grasp of the ownership of the legacy? I'm only saying that not to put down John Lewis but just to say that when older people whom were a part of the black freedom movement of the '60's, [when they] ignore the black freedom movement of today, it infuriates me. And when old SDS people are longing nostalgically for a ship that already left the shore, I want to drop off a bridge. What the fuck is wrong with you? This is happening now. I was at a sit-in last year and some local newsman recognized me and came up to me and said, "Are you mentoring these young people?" Get the fuck out of here! I'm not mentoring these young people. They're mentoring me! And look, I'm not saying history doesn't matter and your experience doesn't matter but partly the whole notion of generations in our quick and hurry up modern world — I'm from the generation of the '60's — wait a minute, I was born in 1944. So I was a part of the generation of the '50's the '70's, the '90's, I'm right here. In fact, the '60's is commodified and sold as a myth and a symbol so it's like, what were the '60's like? Well, there was no such thing as the '60's if you were living there. Nobody lives by decades. No one looked at their watch on December 31, 1969 and said "oh shit, I got to go get high!" Nobody does that. And any realistic look at it — when did the Montgomery bus incident happen? 1956. When was the Supreme Court decision? '54. When were the Freedom Rides and so on and what happened in '73, '71 and '75? I mean, when did Kent State happen? So, I think power uses the '60's, and the popularization of it becomes a wet blanket on young people today, a kind of suppression of clarity and activism. For years people would say to me, I was born in the wrong decade." And I'd say, "No, you weren't, you were born when you were born." And we were as fucked-up and backward as anybody I know, confused and so on. So, I don't want to claim any mentorship but yes, I do want to claim that I'm a part of it. I have my SDS membership still — I never quit — and on our little membership card it says "we are people of this generation, bred in modest comfort, looking uneasily at the world we inherit." That's as true of me today as it was 50 years ago. I'm still a member of this generation, and whatever the so-called "60's" was, it's prelude to much deeper and much more profound changes that we're not only going to need but that we're seeing the wrinkles of right now. It's a pretty exciting time to be alive and I for one plan to be on the barricades no matter what.

There's a great political consciousness out there right now. People are saying, "look, we understand that there are 60 million people whom have voted into office people with a lot of bigotry and a lot of hatred, that they wear on their sleeves." And I think there's a real consciousness that those people exist, and the conversation has turned to the need for resistance, through art and in other ways. I'm wondering if people will get to that ability to teach and to learn or if it's just popular candy.

It's exciting, thrilling — and terrifying. I don't think there's anyway to predict. I'll tell you, I've spent absolutely zero time trying to understand people whom voted for Trump because I don't think it's as important as the pundits have it. One of the things I find fascinating ... the Democratic party and, frankly, the *New York Times*, NPR and other established liberal forces are in no position to form an opposition. One hopes they could find the backbone to do it. But they're in no position to because we've had 4 decades of bipartisan effort that's gotten us mass incarceration, permanent war, the destruction of the public, especially public schools and public housing and an ideology of me, me, me. That's bipartisan. So, what's happening now with the *New York Times* and the Democratic party is they're scrambling to catch up with what's on the street. So they're trying to figure out "how do I manage this, how do I bring it into my party?" and no one knows where that's going to go.

Yes, they want to instrumentalize people.

Absolutely, so here's one example of what you're seeing: the Democratic party has been unable to utter the words "working class" for 40 years and the day after the election, they suddenly discovered that there's a white working class. And you're like, "Dude! Where did you come from." And they're like, "in Michigan the white working class has agreed." and you're like, "Oh, great. How's the black working class doing in Michigan, motherfucker?" You know, it's so stupid and so white supremacist but that's what they're struggling to get ahold of instead. I know that people vote for so many contradictory and crazy reasons that I'm not even going to go there, but I will say that Trump ran explicitly a fascist campaign and that's a different thing from who voted for him and why they voted for him. He ran a fascist campaign. Certainly, it was already beginning to cohere, but he gave it energy — I mean, the Obama moment began to cohere a white supremacist base but Trump gave it energy and direction . So that's what he did — whether Joe Shmoe voted for him or not I don't care.

Right, they just want the trains to run on time.

Yeah. And now what we're seeing is an attempt to consolidate that fascist base and we'll see if the *New York Times* has the spine to stand in opposition. At this point I'd say the record is mixed. On the one hand, they were pretty good about a couple of things early on, especially defending their own turf but then he gave this completely right-wing speech in front of Congress that had all the wrong things in it including creating a force to target immigrants whom commit crimes — that's fascism. And the *New York Times* said he looked presidential. What the fuck are you talking about? I mean, that's the thing if it's just a performance, if it's just optics. But it's not just optics and this is where you can't trust the liberal media and the Democratic party — they're the party of diversity and multiculturalism and not justice. So, do I want optics when it comes to race in this country, or do I really want justice? If I want justice, the Democratic party is not my party. I mean, there are black people in it, I'm not going to disdain it completely or avoid it completely but I'm not going to say that Rahm Emanuel is my guy as opposed to Bruce Rauner, they're both not my guy. And Rauner is better on the optics, he would never use the n-word, but he closes 50 schools [on the south side] and lays off thousands of teachers — yes, that's racism. Structural racism.

When you talk about journalism, as someone who's sometimes a member of that sea of people, it seems to me we're potentially, hopefully, facing a moment like we did after McCarthyism when there was a new willingness to include an analysis of ideology like they hadn't had to do before. The whole idea of objectivity shifted after McCarthy, and part of my hope here is that there's another shift where journalists are willing to go further bring some criticality to the lack of ideology.

Right, let's judge them on that. Let's hold them to that. For example, you may have seen last night that Trump tweeted about Obama phone tapping him. Brand new. So, Trump went nuts and he has access to classified information, he knows what's there and he said, "Obama had my wires tapped at Trump tower," and he says, "this is McCarthyism!" Nobody in a position of power can use the word McCarthyism accurately referring to themselves. McCarthyism was an attack on the working class, on working class people, on the freedom movement —

And on artists.

And on artists! Very much so. But what he's saying is, and it may be true that the Obama administration had their wires tapped but if they did, they had to get a FISA warrant, it wasn't some sneaky operation, we'll see what comes of that. But the point is that McCarthyism may be in the air but the idea that Trump could be the victim of McCarthyism is insane.

That's Trump's old mentor Roy Cohn's reversal tactics at play.

Absolutely, he's very clear on that. Anyway, so I think it is a period where journalism could find its center again, its soul again. But the only thing I'm clear on is that historically progress in this country comes from fire from below. And real change can't come without regular politics, so I often say we have to walk toward revolution and walk toward socialism on two legs. One leg is the constant mobilization of people and that mobilization could take many forms and the other leg is real politics that can respond to that. My example would be Lyndon Johnson, a cracker from Texas, passed the most far-reaching civil rights legislation since Reconstruction and he did it because of the pressure of fire from below, not because he had a change of mind all of a sudden. I mean, he was an effective politician who could respond — Abraham Lincoln, the same thing. Never belonged to an Abolitionist party, in fact if you read Lincoln's first inaugural, it's genuflecting in front of the slave owners, it's saying "we won't disturb your enterprise, don't worry about us." And 4 years later? My God, Frederick Douglas could have written the second inaugural, and that's the one you see in the history books. Nobody reads the first inaugural. If you see a compilation of historical documents, it's the second inaugural. Not the first, the first is shameful. And so, it's true of FDR too. He wasn't a part of the labor movement. But he responded to the labor movement. So I think in the last 30-40 years the problem we've had is that when young people are pulled into politics, they're pulled into an election. And an election is the least of it — electoral politics is something and it's not unimportant, but to have it be the center of a change strategy misses the absolute importance not just at the beginning but throughout that people are mobilized, organized and activated collectively. So, without that--this is one that just really irks me. If you read a textbook about legal stuff you will come across the idea the 1954 Supreme Court decision [Brown v. Board of Education] unleashed decades of activism, and what that fails to say is that decades of activism lead to the 1954 Supreme Court decision. What changed these 9 guys' minds? Why did Plessy V. Ferguson suddenly become not good? The idea that they just sat there and suddenly said "hey, I have an idea, Plessy v. Ferguson sucks!" I'm at the age where — I don't know if you read Betsy DeVos's statement about the historically black colleges. She's sitting in a meeting with the presidents of the HBCU's and she says, "the HBCU's are pioneers in the movement for choice in education." What?! Black colleges were a choice? They were actually a response to segregation, "you wouldn't let us in, motherfucker," and she's like, "choice works!"

It's so insane.

They don't think of people as legitimate paths to power, they only respect money.

It's what they believe in. We live in crazy times. The other thing I was going to say was that I was going to Washington on January 19 to be part of a peace demonstration against Hillary Clinton — we organized it last summer. And had Hillary Clinton gotten elected, it would have been a normal transition — I would have been here, you would have been there, nobody would have had to think too deeply about it. Eh, "don't be a warmonger, motherfucker." And we would have all been in our places. What Trump does is he creates the conditions where everyone, including me, has to rethink everything and that's what this one writer named Jack Halberstam calls the "queer art of failure." The idea is when your relationship is going along, your career is going along, you don't have to think about much deeply. You still think but you're not challenged. But then when something goes wrong you have to think about everything, you have to go back to the roots — why did we fall in love? How did that happen? Where did we start to fuck up?

Why am I on fire right now?

Exactly. It's a great moment. I don't ever want to say there's a silver lining to a fascist regime, I won't say it. But what I will say is that the election of Trump forced all of us to wonder at a deeper level how we got here and where we're going. For a lot of us, me included, I see the roots of it going back into the '80's, I see the acceleration of white supremacy in 2008 — a coherent white supremacy — white supremacy was always there and I see a kind of anesthetizing response from the Democratic party as Bill Clinton put in welfare reform and criminal justice reform and mass incarceration and all the things that went with that, all with the optics of inclusion but not with the ideology of justice. And I think that's what we all have to rethink now and wonder about.

"We come together to unleash our wild and free

imaginations — our art and humor and creative energies — to defeat the plodding, murderous and instrumentalist logic of war. Theirs is a calculus of conquest and pain. Ours offers a measure of healing and possibility." This passage is particularly interesting to me because all of this conversation happened right after the election, artists came out and said, "I'm going to make art!"

> Isn't that brilliant? Isn't it the best?

I think it's exactly my belief system. But this is the question. Is art an effective political tool and if so, how can it be most effective? Is it just a facile response? like just showing up to protests and taking selfies because you look cool with the bandana mask on? Clearly, there's the benefit of a visible community, the affirmation of that. But how can art be a tool or is it just a kind of candy to feel like you're doing something?

> I'm not an artist except of my own life, which everybody is.

That's of consequence.

> Yeah, that's not nothing. If you see is yourself as an artist in your own life it matters, but my admiration for musicians, for poets, visual artists and painters is over the top and part of the reason is that I tend to be more didactic in my organizing

and speaking — in spite of myself, I tend to be more telling than imagining. And I think what's brilliant about the arts and about humor, is that it's generous in a way that didactics can never be generous, that it always involves listening and performing or listening and speaking, it always involves a relationship. I remember speaking in Minnesota many, many years ago, I think I was probably in my 20's, and an audience member said to me — and I thought I'd given a pretty careful talk about war and peace — and the first question was, "why do you think you're better than me?" And I hadn't said anything about being better than anybody. But there's something about a didactic speech that sounds superior and there's something about the arts that invites you in so we can all laugh together about stuff that we have a hard time hearing if it seems accusatory. So for example, this is why I think Jon Stewart was so effective, where I think Trevor Noah can become very effective. Because they're able to get you laughing and then thinking and if they're able to get you laughing and thinking in a way together then somebody who maybe felt put on the defensive, "why are you a racist?" — it's not actually the right way to start a conversation. Whereas sending up — I remember my dad with me the last 5 years of his life and he had Alzheimer's and sometimes I'd come home from work and he'd be listening to Fox news on full volume and I'd have to turn it down and one day I came home and turned it down and he said, "Bill, what do these gay people want?" And I said, "Well, they don't want to marry you but let me show you something," and then I showed him a cartoon in the *New Yorker* of two dogs walking down the street and one is saying to the other, "Just because he stroked your ear and you liked it doesn't mean you're gay." Now, that's fucking *hilarious*. That's better than me saying, "It's human right, motherfuckers!" I'll give you a couple of examples. I don't know if you saw Karim Sulayman's 1-man performance [with filmmaker Meredith Kaufman Younger] on Central Park south, right after the election but he's a guy who went to Lab School with my kids. 35- or 37-year old opera singer in New York, very dark skin very tall and he went in front of the Trump tower in Central Park South and he had a big sign that said "My name is Karim Sulayman, I am a Muslim and I'm worried and I want to know whom here will stand with me?" He put on a blindfold and he stood there opera singing and he just stood there, vulnerable just absolutely vulnerable with a sign and his voice. People were skeptical at first and then somebody came up and hugged him.

Man, how do you not respond to that?

My God. Before it was over, there was not a dry eye in the house. People were putting their kids up next to him and saying "here, kiss my baby." Shit like that. I mean, that was an art intervention that speaks volumes. And I've seen many, many others like that over the last few months which boggle my mind.

Well, and you mention the 1980's which were the nationally and internationally visible moment where the GOP and Reagan, at the same time they were restricting Visas and travel for people with HIV and A.I.D.S., they were shutting down performance artists whom were talking about it in the arts that were funded by the N.E.A., so they didn't want those messages going out and I think in that way there's a real quashing of dissent through the arts that can happen. To the degree that imagination is a political act — if you're imagining worlds other than the one they want you to inhabit — that's something they want to silence.

Some. But, some not. And see, my plea is to unleash our radical imaginations. And another way I sometimes think about it is, it's a plea to release our social imaginations. It's both more than castles in the clouds, but it's also important to remember that Auschwitz was an incredible act of imagination. You and I couldn't have thought of that, we don't have that imaginative capacity, nor do we have —

The hatred.

Right, we don't have any of that going for us. But

our social imaginations, our radical imaginations of
a world that could be but is not yet, a world where
everyone's in and no one's out — that world we
can also imagine. All the forward progress we've
ever seen is an act of wild imagination, typically
in a social world that promoted it. So that's why
the plea for the imagination and that is reason
enough to admire and dive in and pay attention
to the arts. Long before Hamilton was what it is,
what I loved was the idea that you could rethink
the Founding Fathers and, if you think about it for
a minute, these were a bunch of hungry, scrappy
young kids and to reimagine them as black and
Latin meeting in a room above a bar, what a great
fucking image.

Right, which is what we should be able to do.

We should be able to do and that's why, coming
at the Black Lives Matter moment it has a differ-
ent resonance. Kerry James Marshall's show at the
Museum of Contemporary Art in Chicago coming
at the Black Lives Matter moment, it was like —
whoa! It speaks to, reflects, amplifies something
unbelievable.

Yes, and this notion of Chicago that Ta-Nehisi
Coates mentions as the center of black American
culture, with BY100 as the roots out of which Black
Lives Matter emerged, I think there's something
of an interesting convergence in the city of racial

politics and racial culture and then looking back at the social practice history that informs it going back 100 years to Hull House and Jane Addam's invention of social work, Chicago's an exciting place to be working in the realm of all these ideas as an extension of the avant garde history that was insulated against the neoliberalism that absorbed it in the culture of the coastal bubbles.

> I agree, and then you have Chance the Rapper, who's a student of Kevin Coval, Eve Ewing, all these incredible people who come out of the Louder Than a Bomb thing, which is incredible in itself. Then you see things like BY100, Undocumented and Unafraid, which came out of UIC. That's where it was born. It was born by a group of students whose parents always told them "Shh, you're going to Lane Tech, you're going to university but don't tell anybody about us." Then suddenly they meet each other at UIC and they're like, "fuck this. I'm undocumented, I'm unafraid." Then the 2005 march from the west side to the Loop, looping by the Haymarket statue. What a wonderful confluence. So, we're lucky, just like the characters in Hamilton to say, "how lucky are we to be alive right here right now?" That's how I feel. How lucky am I to be a part of this generation? I always remind people that everyone you're seeing here, you and me and everyone else will be dead in 100 years. So it's worth remembering that even though it seems like something that I'm an old

person, you're a middle-aged person, it's not true. We're all here and we're all a part of the same generations and it's important to not that we're all here and moving through history and history's being made and we've seen history surprise us before and it can surprise us again. And that's a message I want to keep in my own mind, that we can be the agents of that change.

Jeez Loueez [32]

Thanks for taking the time to talk with me today.

> I'm originally from St Louis. My dad's a musician and a singer, and he plays drums and keyboard, and my mom was always doing plays and poetry and dancing. But that's the end of it in my family, no one else in my family is really artistic.

So, a little bit of the black sheep syndrome?

> Yes. I started taking dancing when I was 5, I really wanted to do it and my grandmother on my dad's side started taking me the classes and would say, "get her to do something." Then I just loved it. So, I started when I was 5, but then later wanted to quit dancing because I was like, "I want to be in a band. I want to play trumpet now," so I started playing trumpet and keyboard." I was in a jazz

32   Originally published at *Art Intercepts*, Dec. 20, 2017, http://www.artintercepts. org/2017/12/20/movement-matters-an-interview-with-jeez-loueez.

band, but I didn't like it. I wantßed to be in a band of some kind, but I didn't want to specifically be a jazz musician, which was just random, and out of left field. So, then I went back, in high school, to dancing and acting. I was in all the spring musicals and in all the plays, and I was dancing, and I was in a jazz band, and on the tennis team. I was all of those things. I love that dancing can encompass musicality, you know, I love music so much, and even though I might not be playing music so much, I can use my body as an instrument and tell a story without using a word, I can take you to the resolution of a story like that. My thing is the standard Jazz, tap, ballet, my top 3.

And so, when does this community dance side of it come in for you? social dance?

In middle school and high school, I kind of hung in the back a little bit, I wasn't in the middle of the circle. It was still sort of stressing me out. Especially if everyone knows you're a dancer, they're all like, "Ohh, you better bring it." But I love going out and dancing. Now I'm definitely less self-conscious, I love going to dance clubs.

Is that something that started in St. Louis, going around to dance clubs and night spots?

That was more in Chicago. I was still more of a teenager in St. Louis. I came to Chicago to go to

Columbia College in 2005 to study musical the-
atre. Because in musical theatre, you can combine
dancing and singing and acting. For the longest
time I was like, "I'm going to go to Juilliard!" But
they didn't have what I was looking for, you had
to pick and I didn't feel like I wanted to have to
pick. Columbia College has open enrollment so
anybody can get in. I got a little money, a few
grand and I came to Chicago. My first profes-
sor there was Sheldon Patinkin, and he was the
biggest influence. I feel like up until I went to
college I didn't really know what theater was, I
didn't really know enough about it. We had things
like drama class in high school but I hadn't really
had any theatre background or training. It was a
very eye-opening experience. I was like, "what is
happening?" Stephanie Shaw was a huge influ-
ence and she cast me in my first play there. That's
where I met people like Po'chop there — Cruel
Valentine, who is on the board of Jeezy's Juke
Joint, I met in keyboarding class. I started doing
burlesque while I was still in school. I graduated
in 2010 and had started performing in 2009. I
had a friend who was in a burlesque troupe and
I'd been working strip clubs. Somebody dropped
out of their show, and they needed somebody last
minute. This was a troupe called the Ripettes. They
literally needed a last-minute replacement, and I
was like, "I'll do it!" and I've been doing burlesque
ever since. I love that I can do musical theater and
combine that with my love of stripping, I loved

the fact that I was in control of my own narrative, character-making, in control of how I dress and photographing myself and not having to fit into other people's feeling about me so much.

When did you start stripping?

I went to my first amatuer night when I was 19. Then I started working regularly at this club in Chicago in 2008. Every venue is different, there's theaters, there's nightclubs, with burlesque shows the audience knows it's art, knows what to expect — it's also adult entertainment, but it's also art. It's different at nightclubs, it's different performing in gay bars than in straight bars. I was way more shy and self-conscious about my body when I first started doing this, when I started doing burlesque. I thought it was for voluptuous women with an hourglass figure and nice shoes. and I was like, "I don't have a pin-up body." People say shit all the time. So I was very nervous about taking my clothes off, even though I'd already worked in the strip club, there was this time I was performing for an HRC event and this woman in the crowd was basically saying that my body was gross and too skinny. I was like, "First of all, I can hear you bitch. You're right there, I can hear you."

This was coming out of another woman's mouth?

Yes! People have been saying rude things from

before when I started performing, and so it defi-
nitely made me feel more positive, and people
who have my body type say, "Thank you so much!
When you come out there, I never thought I could
do burlesque, and I see you doing it and it makes
me feel better now.

It's sounds like there's notable difference for you per-
forming for a white crowd versus an audience that's
majority of people of color?

Yeah, and the only real differences depend on the
story you're trying to tell. Especially if I'm hosting,
and I'm hosting in front of an all white audience,
it's going to be a different deal. But when I started
doing this I was like, "Where all the people of
color performers at?" I wanted to know all the
burlesque legends, and the one they always tell you
about is Josephine Baker, and she's amazing but
she wasn't the only black burlesque performer ever
in life. But, a lot of that history has been erased,
so I started my blog, interviewing people trying to
preserve that history and then I said there should
be a show, let's start a show. That's how Jeezy's Juke
Joint was born.

Daniel Bozutzky [33]

Your newest book just came out, called *Lake Michigan*, and I've seen it described as the Homan Square section of the codex it's been suggested you're working on. Is that a fair assessment?

> So, at the end of my last book, the *Performance of Becoming Human*, there are some pieces that take place in a prison site on the beach in Chicago and so this becomes a kind of continuation of that project. On one level, it's thinking about Homan Square and police violence in Chicago more broadly — I'll just say that — so Homan Square is certainly a part of it, but I think the interest is certainly broader than that.

There's this interesting dividing line in the work that I think of as this reality of thought versus imagination, or poetry and politics, which I feel people often

33   Originally published at *Newcity,* March 12, 2018, https://lit.newcity.com/2018/03/12/the-conversation-the-sound-and-rhythm-of-poet-daniel-borzutzky.

say don't go together, but I see them as inseparable
in some of my favorite poetry. In a sense, they have
the same goals.

> So, the poetry is all political and responding to the
> various political and economic realities of our time,
> and I would say two things: I wouldn't have the
> pretensions to confuse poetry with policy, and so
> to that degree, it's not attempting to do that, but I
> think part of the problem with that question is that
> it seems you can't have the one without the other,
> and certainly I'm using features of poetic language
> and narrative throughout the book. There's all kind
> of dialogues with other writers, there is repetition
> throughout the book of an interest in sound and
> rhythm, and all of those things are certainly sepa-
> rate from what you would do in an essay.

The follow-up to that question for me then is always,
doesn't that suggest there's something wrong with
art for art's sake? Doesn't that make it a politically
problematic stance to take, to reject the inclusion
of politics in art and I think about your work, it
would be impossible for your work to exist without
it, without the politics.

> To the degree that I don't want to tell anybody
> what they should do with their art — I would start
> there — but I would also say that rejecting politics
> or doing art for art's sake is also political, right?
> It's an approach to how you think about politics

in relationship to what's going on in our society,
or to what you *think* is going on in our society,
that that's then also a stance.

And I don't think we can talk about your poetry then,
without talking about Zurita. You are a longtime
translator of his work, and in *Song for His Disap-
peared Love*, much as in your work throughout the
last few books, there is this sort of imagined country
that intervenes on that outside, quote-unquote real
world that poses this call for love in response to vio-
lence or tyranny. Is that a viable parallel argument
that can be made about what's happening in your
work?

Maybe some in *Performance of Becoming
Human*, I'm not sure I see that optimism in
Lake Michigan.

Mm. There's this anger or *outrage* about what's
happening that's very visceral in your work that I
wholeheartedly appreciate, and would like to see
more of in our art-making out there in the world.

I think in terms of imagining a country or a nation,
I think it's doing a couple things: on the one hand,
thinking about what is already happening, to some
degree under the surface, or that is not entirely
visible, so something like Homan Square which
literally was invisible — well, I shouldn't say lit-
erally — but which was invisible to *most* of us,

but then I have also been thinking about those things that are scarcely visible and drawing them out to their logical conclusions, right? And so, it comes across throughout the books in terms of state violence and treatment of immigrants, and in terms of economic policy, it's thinking about what we know is happening but we don't sort of panic about, and trying to push that to where I think it's heading, and that's what I think people don't see.

Right, and with these historical precedents, for instance, talking about Pinochet as one of the original neoliberals, do you see that as a sort of parallel between what was happening in Chile and what's happening now, what you refer to often in the text as a corpse, or a carcass economy?

Yes so, starting around 2014, I started to write a lot about what was happening in the relationship between Chile and Chicago, which I was thinking of then mostly in economic terms, and the experiments that the Chicago Boys and Milton Friedman wanted to enact in terms of privatizations that were done in Chile, and at extreme levels, and that serve as a model because all these ideas were being tested out. So, Chile has this sort of privatization on a mass level of schools, healthcare, social security, and so in 2012 when the Chicago Public Schools were on strike for the first time in 27 years, I think, in Chile they were in the midst of a year-long student strike, their issues were largely the same. Their issues were about privatization, and access. So I was certainly thinking about parallels; Chile uses a voucher system to supplement people's ability to pay for private education as a way of crushing public education, which is what has been proposed recently when George Bush wanted to privatize social security, he talked about Chile as being the model for that, and claimed it was successful. But so, I think there are all these economic policies and I think the idea that it begins in Chicago and then moves to Chile is central, so it's all important to me as a Chilean living in Chicago, but I like to bring it back because I think the endgame is to bring it back to Chicago and the U.S., and in Chile, those policies were sustained by repression and state violence. While I'm very careful to not say that Chicago and Chile are the same thing, or that the way violence has worked is the same — of course in Chile, the numbers of people who died or were tortured are much greater — I would say that state violence, and especially abuses toward poor and minority communities, that they are used as a means of sustaining public policies that seek to rid those communities of social and public services.

Rahm's closing down 60 public schools on Chicago's south side, for instance.

Right, but which is happening at the same time as cops are killing kids on the south side, and I think that's the point I want to make, is that those are *not separate things*. That the killing of black youth on the south side serves as a means of sustaining the policies of shutting down those schools.

Yes, maintenance of this sort of systemic, endemic program of oppression. It strikes me that Zurita was also a performance artist, staging actions in the streets. It's interesting to me. Is that something you were thinking of when you were writing the *Performance of Becoming Human*, this sort of action, is it something that was there, and influencing how you were writing and thinking about it?

No, I was thinking about performance, but not so much in the sense of this kind of art action. The title refers back, for me, to this story by Kafka, *A Report to an Academy*, which is about an African ape who is captured, put in chains and taken back, and tortured on the ship, and in order to find his way out, he begins to act like the humans on the ship. They're really vile, they spit and belch all the time, and he begins to imitate them, and then finally learns how to talk and goes around Europe giving speeches on his transformation. But he, the ape, while he's plotting how to imitate or ape the humans, he begins to speak as an artistic performance, right? So that was the seed, but it got me to thinking about the various ways that we perform humanity, on the one hand to survive — that's one kind of performance that people have

to do, but on the other hand — in all of our sort
of various social situations, right? — I'm thinking
particularly about the way that people with power
choose to perform or not perform their humanity
... is kind of central.

Correct, humanity is a choice.

Yeah, and I think Kafka's point, and then, I refer-
ence in *Lake Michigan*, Aimé Césaire's point, is
that the choice that humans, and often civilized
humans make, is to act like barbarians. And they
do that through systemic violence and killing of
people who have less *power* than they do.

You've described neoliberalism as a resurgent force,
particularly in Chicago, can you elaborate on how
you see that unfolding?

I think I'm precisely talking about those poli-
cies of public education, but not limited to that
issue, I think we see all sorts of ways in which the
public sector is affected, that the city government
is deciding to disinvest in public services, to hand
that over, be that through the closing of schools
or mental health facilities or [privatization of]
prisons, to street and utility services, so there's all
kinds of ways in which Chicago would hand over
its responsibilities to private companies.

It's interesting to me, this veering-off that's

happened. At a certain point historically, markets became a solution to these martial ways of thinking, these militaristic ways of thinking in which the combat ethic was everything, and through which interpersonal and national conflicts were resolved *largely* through violent contest and bloodshed. Markets and commerce, in that sense, eventually garnered the power to dictate priorities for military engagement in a way that broke the dominant hold of widespread violence over interactions in society. Now, they've been pushed to this extreme, where the thinking is that we can instrumentalize and monetize everything, right down to people's sense of individuality. So there's the split between the two branches of history that takes us from Pinochet and Milton Friedman and all this, and in the poetry I think you see these things coming together to the point where you're holding up these bloody hands and saying, "Look, you should be ashamed! This is what you have done!"

> Is there a point to be made or balance to account for the sense that markets can be seen as somehow less nefarious? Umm. *No.* Because we don't have a lot of empirical evidence at the moment — so, okay. The ideology that is purported by neoliberals is that market economics will trickle down through competition and through job creation in order to benefit the public, and people who do not have money.

Yes, and on a fundamental level markets are a negation of collective action.

> Sure, we simply don't have enough evidence — again, if we take Chicago as the example, we simply don't have enough evidence that there is much interest in market investment in sustaining low income communities. Opening up a Whole Foods in poor neighborhoods is not an act which is going to end with real investment in what those neighborhoods need, and one could argue that doing things like that becomes the first step in removing low income people from the neighborhood, right? So, no, to that degree I simply don't see it. And again, if we toggle back and forth between Chile and Chicago, the question of whom markets benefit, it's simply: the markets benefits people who can afford to be invested in them and who can control profit and the means of production. I just don't see it. I just don't see … Chile has been using this slogan lately of "Capitalism with a human face" as an idea that could provide a counterbalance to some of the neoliberal ideas that were in place, but it's not addressing the abandonment and social cruelties that mass Capitalism and neoliberalism have created.

Yes, it's this sort of extremism that you're trying to root out in this experience of the two worlds.

> Yes, except the extremism is mainstream, right?

It is extreme, except Rahm Emanuel runs as a liberal Democrat. Chile, since the end of the coup has had three socialist presidents and they still have a mostly privatized school and healthcare and social security system. So, the idea is that these very right-wing policies both in the U.S., and in Chile have become simply the center, and to some degree, the center left.

And centered on these sort of death-cult approaches to economics, really. Do you then see these works as a critique of Modernity? Its successes and failures, the disillusionment that has come along with it, and the social cruelties that have been manufactured out of it?

I mean, just to limit the scope of the question a little bit, I think I would say that it's a critique of the way in which — I don't know, I don't know if I'm critiquing Modernity in my writing, but I am critiquing the ways in which market forces and mass Capitalism have existed side-by-side with extreme violence, with genocide, with racism and oppression throughout the U.S., and that they are forces that simply run parallel. To that degree, that's a facet of Modernity, yes.

Right, so now with the emergence of Trumpism and the collusion of the far-right, and of the right in general in many ways, the full range of bigotries and devaluation of humanity is on display. And I think

then, in some sense, that if there's any art form that
has any effective capacity to work against all that,
it's poetry, right? Do you think it has that capacity
to push back in a real way against these narratives
of exploitation and oppression?

> Yes. That's right. I would say two things. I would
> say, stepping again outside of the United States
> and thinking about the ways in which writers and
> artists in South America and Latin America have
> sought to affect the public sphere through art, I
> think that that is an ideal, well, that that is a value
> that has existed for for many writers and artists
> who have lived under dictatorships. I think that
> poetry and literature in general are so marginalized
> that the question of audience is inevitably really
> limited, and I think that as a writer, I'm always
> struggling against the idea of wanting to write in
> such a way as to participate in a public narrative,
> or in a public dialogue, or to have my work com-
> menting on what's going on in the public, and
> knowing that that is extremely limited. But I think
> the writers who I admire most felt very devoted
> to that idea, right? That their writing should be
> in conversation with a public, that it should have
> some service in inspiring social thought and action
> in some way.

Right, that it have some direct intentionality about
its social relevance.

It's a kind of dual ambivalence, of knowing the
limitations and wanting to imagine the possibil-
ities for that.

Rosé Hernandez [34]

You're originally from Dallas, correct? What brought
you to Chicago?

Yes, I'm originally from Dallas, and came here on
a transfer. I have this huge art history and theater
background, but I stepped away from the theater
because there were no roles for me. There aren't
any roles for Latinos in plays and especially in
my interest: classical theater, classical training.
I applied to School of the Art Institute and it
seemed like the best fit. I was working with video
and got back into performance. It was a different
approach because it was me making performance
work and figuring out what that would look like,
toiling around making these mimic-y works draw-
ing on seventies body art, very body-based. Lots
of Chris Burden stuff, and then I thought, "this

34   Originally published at *Newcity*, July 9, 2016, https://www.newcitystage.
com/2016/07/09/exit-the-void-rose-hernandezs-luscious-queer-transit.

> just feels weird." It felt like I was back again in someone else's play. It was when I started working with Ginger Krebs and got into her work, she kind of mentored me and was a huge influence on me. I was thinking about applying different sorts of philosophy practices — we were reading The Plague of Fantasies by Zizek who now, eight years later, I'm kind of like okay, wow.

Right, the Judson Church era, all of it was driven into the background by a deep fascination with Postmodernism and poststructuralist theory.

> Definitely, and I was also learning a lot from looking at Minimalist sculpture and thinking about mind, body, performance, presence and the act of viewing — which is when my theatrical training came back in. My work got bigger, more theatrical, bringing in a lot from the audience and my own experience, growing up queer and Latino in Texas, and just even a fat, goth teen. I grew up really Catholic too, and moved away from that as a teenager, and got into witchcraft and the occult. I was like, "why isn't this in my work?" and reading a lot of performance theory, specifically by [Richard] Schechner and thinking a lot about cultural studies, different tribes, and ritual practices in different cultures, and creating my own practices and ritual urbanism. I got taken with it and went into a more specifically spiritual practice.

Tell me about working with Ron Athey and the work you've done showing out in Los Angeles, it seems you've had a stronger reception there than in Chicago.

I've been a fan of Athey's for a number of years and a lot of my influences come from that era of late eighties performance artists. He came to Chicago to perform a few years ago at Mana, through Joseph Ravens and Defibrillator Gallery, and Joseph said, "I've got to clean up the place, they all want to hang out and meet some artists." So, basically we just hung out all night with Ron and Jon John and Sage Charles. We talked a lot about our own work and where we came from and made the connection that way over three days. Ron talked about us with Manuel Vason, the photographer who works with all these different performance artists all over the world. We were in his performance during Rapid Pulse last year. When I went to L.A. he asked me if I wanted to perform at a club or a gallery. I told him I wanted the trip to really be worth it, and that's how I met Nacho Nava who hosts the biggest queer party in L.A. called "Mustache Mondays." Before all that, Ron put up this photo of me on his Facebook and said, "this person is coming to L.A., give them a show." And that's how I got in touch with Jennifer Doyle who curated music and performances at Human Resources. I performed at the MOCA-Geffen; I was in Wisconsin at ACRE, they drove me to

Madison and I basically had one day to get ready.

One of the performances I saw of yours at High Concept Labs involved destroying a sculpture, literally tearing it to pieces and crushing it with your body.

> I wish people didn't have to think of art objects as precious all the time. And also, destruction is a creative force in its own right, too. We went into that performance knowing we were going to destroy a sculpture — that was with my collaborative team called Burning Orchid that I'm in with my friend Efrén Arcoiris and he's like, "I'm just going to build you something and I want you to destroy it, just fuck it up and sit on it." And I said "okay, I'll sit on it." That performance was insane because it was almost an installation in that white warehouse space, and I was plastered against the wall. I said "I'm going to be in this corner, not moving for thirty minutes and I just want you to throw a bucket of plaster on me." So I was really stuck to the wall. At one point I peeled off from the architecture of the space and made my way toward this stupa with all these stations and five different parts of different elements and with a giant void at the top.

It's interesting you walked away from your earlier Catholicism and yet still ended up with a spiritual practice.

Catholicism is really fucked up. I think the imagery is so gorgeous and I love the structure of Mass, the timing and the structure of the Mass, how everything has a certain order: you kneel down, you get up. I was thinking about how a lot of that was a performance and that leads into these rituals in other cultures. There are things you do in a certain order: "this is where we stand." You have to do it in a certain way and then you throw in the leaves, throw in the salt and then you walk three times around this way. So, there's all these different kinds of movements and rules you're inventing to build this ritual. Urban ritual — I did say that. You know, I'm living in a city and there are certain things I do. I'm getting up, setting an alarm. I have to make it to this bus at a certain time. What is the weather like outside? That decides what shoes I wear, what jacket I put on. Who do I run into on the street? All of these things that help you get through your life — it's like, "I'm going to get my coffee because I need this," or "I'm going to get my juice," it's these certain things I need to get through my day. Or, things that I do to wind down. "I have to go have this beer," or "I have to go have this gin and tonic." So these things we do, there's simple silly self-care things and things you do to make you feel safe living in the city, because the city is a really fucked up place.

Right, and people can be really fucked up to each other.

Right, it's capitalism and people are bullshit. People build their own safe spaces for themselves to deal with wanting to lash out and rage — which I also think is healthy too. It's important to build-in yourself that time to tune in and drop out.

Young Jean Lee

If you consider your work in any way a response to
your own personal experiences with racism, sexism or
other bigotries, do you think that it or the dialogue it
may inspire changes the minds of racists and sexists
at all? Please elaborate.

In my mind, pretty much everyone qualifies as a "racist" or "sexist," just to varying degrees. I have had people tell me that my work changed their minds. For example, in my show *THE SHIPMENT*, a character explains why calling a black person the n-word is not the same thing as calling a white person a cracker. Someone told me that after seeing the show, they changed their minds about that particular issue. But since I don't write "message" shows, they aren't really designed to change people's minds. I think they're more designed to shake up people's customary ways of thinking and get them to question themselves, which in my experience often leads to decreased bigotry.

Do you think people feel like your work presents a
threat to how they think of themselves in terms of
race, gender or otherwise?

> For some people, definitely. But in my experience,
> the thing people always find the most threatening
> is formal deviation from convention. Non-linearity,
> lack of climax in an ending, nonsensical language.
> There's something about formal experimentation
> that hits a lot of people in a primal spot that makes
> them intensely angry and uncomfortable. When
> I did my show *CHURCH* in Colorado Springs,
> which had a lot of surrealistic language in it, all
> the Christians in the audience were more freaked
> out by the language and structure of the play than
> by the content. There's something about that con-
> ventional narrative — the lone hero (usually male)
> pursues his singular goal, defeating obstacles until
> he gets his way — that is very important to people.

Do you think this cultural dialogue influences ide-
ology at all? How so?

> It has definitely influenced my personal ideology,
> as well as that of others. As for ideology that forms
> the basis of political or economic policy, I have no
> idea. The impact of the arts on structural injustice
> is a mystery to me.

Claire Tancons[35]

Long since branded an insular realm defined by extensive histories of structural classism and sexism, the international art world also has come increasingly under public fire in recent years for often cluelessly flaunting its white supremacist leanings. It's become near-impossible to ignore the drumbeat of charges of racism over artworks that have tread, and in many instances openly crossed the line into, increasingly disturbing territory.

White artist Dana Schultz's questionable decision to render a painterly abstraction of Emmett Till's corpse in his open casket at the Whitney Museum in New York comes to mind, following as it had on the outcries of minstrelsy in white artist Joe Scanlon's hired-gun performance of an "invented" black artist named Donelle Woolford. That move that prompted the withdrawal in protest of art collective The Yams to the equivalent of yawns and muted shrugs of "that's just how things work around here" from organizers.

And of course, most recently, the Walker Art Center in

35   Originally published in the *Chicago Tribune*, July 11, 2017.

Minneapolis was forced to withdraw LA-based artist Sam Durant's Scaffold, a replica of a gallows used in the 1862 execution of 38 Dakota Indian males, the largest mass hanging in the history of the United States. The work outcries from members of the Dakota tribe that it celebrates those executions and, even if inadvertent, served to resonate positively with the American genocide of indigenous peoples.

Against this emerging background, understanding the art world's structural blind spots when it comes to race, some artists have been thrust into the spotlight by merit of their forceful responses to it, sweeping aside the gatekeeping conventions of that system where needed. Kerry James Marshall, for instance, has been rightly celebrated not only for the stunning skill and mastery evident throughout his decades of painting but also for the corrections his work delivers to the depictions, or lack thereof, of black people throughout art history.

Painting itself has been transformed by his work. Similarly, as an outgrowth of the historic avant-garde, performance art has become near-unassailably popular in the art world given the historical precedent of the soil out of which it has grown, over the last century, as the first art form to protest the "institution of art," (i.e., the art world) — which its members saw as upholding cruel and even barbarous belief systems encoded in moralized hierarchies of nature as the basic register of their aesthetic virtue. Dadaism, cubism, surrealism, all a product of its purview, have since their founding been uprooted from the social contexts in which they were produced and their value reduced to what sales figures they may fetch at Christie's. Art that is performed then, over as it fades into the receding moment and without producing an object, seems uniquely suited as a perfect vehicle for upending this narrow, traditionalist and even puritanical means of art's valuation.

In addressing this history, *En Mas'* co-curator Claire Tancons goes much further, arguing that there are separate "genealogies of performance in the Caribbean and a genealogy of performance seen through the lens of Europe," as she explains via telephone.

> "There is a defining book on the history of performance art as we know it, within the mainstream art world, if you will, and that is the book (called *Performance Art: From Futurism to the Present*) that was written by Roselee Goldberg, who is widely hailed as the founder, really, of the discipline of performance art.

> "It was written without specifying that it was written from the point of view of the West. It seems to assume and generalize that any and every history of performance would stand on this particular canon, which the author traces back to dada, surrealism, futurism, etc., etc. The work that (co-curator Krista) Thompson and I have done with *En Mas'* is in keeping with this redressing of the Western-centric canon."

In their approach to so doing, they have also sought to provide a corrective to Western-centric notions of exactly what social function carnivals are meant to serve. In that sense, the European history that informs the popular understanding of carnival situates it as an inversion of social hierarchies in which the peasants rule and the monarchs or rulers are, for a short period of time, regarded as members of

the lower classes. Through such inversion, it was
theorized by intellectuals such as Mikhail Bakhtin,
the tensile strength of prevailing social and politi-
cal conventions could be tested and, where needed,
improvements made.

> "Carnival in the Americas is a de facto modern
> phenomenon," Tancons asserts, "and so you have
> to begin thinking of the carnivals of the Americas,
> which includes the Caribbean up to New Orle-
> ans, if you consider New Orleans culturally as a
> Caribbean city, and of course the carnivals of Latin
> America, they are de facto modern practices by
> dint of the legacy of the colonial conquests, slavery,
> the Middle Passage, etc., etc. So we are very much
> questioning, again, the Western notion through
> which carnival theory continues to be applied to
> the Caribbean, though it very clearly applies to a
> different set of circumstances, more of a traditional
> Bakhtinian definition of carnival."

By taking this approach, Tancons and Thompson have charted
a course in the work intended to strip away an invisibility rooted
in racial motivations that views white perspectives as superior to
those of indigenous peoples, and which rolls back the imposition
of a Western historical worldview on how we understand the
avant-garde, performance and art in favor of a more diverse canon.

That diversity seems almost encoded into the DNA of the exhibit
at times, bursting through in the range of colors in the works rep-
resented here, notably in Nicolas Dumit Estevez's documentary

photographs of friends at C Room, an eight-hour performance at the Museo Folklorico Don Tomas Morel in the Dominican Republic. Among those works selected for *En Mas'* are also a number that focus on the act of procession as a key element, such as Jamaican artist Charles Campell, with his Actor Boy: Fractal Engagement, for which he replaced traditional headgear and masks worn during the traditional John Canoe (Or Jonkunno) street tour with spherical, papier-mache cutouts inspired by Buckminster Fuller's geodesic domes.

Perhaps most effective, however, is Marlon Griffith's "Positions+Power," a collection of images, videos and installation that depict a figure wearing a giant helmet for a head, fitted with two large round goggles that project beams of white light. At times the figure is depicted atop a plain wood trellis, surrounded by procession-goers, hand in salute. Simultaneously evoking both the militarized "police booths that are omnipresent at carnival time" and alien invaders, Griffith refers to the character as the Overseer. Accompanied by a watchdog known as the Doberman, the pair are depicted in Jamaican photographer Marlon James' images intervening on the streets of Trinidad. Stripped of their usual Trinidadian accoutrements, the wandering of the small band of artists "takes on the tradition of 'individuals'" by blurring the identity differences between them, and setting the group aside from the mass.

The very title of the exhibition encodes this difference, doubling as it does as short for "masquerade," which is used as short for carnival in the Caribbean, and the French colloquial "en masse," meaning "in a group" or "all together." In effectively puncturing the masquerade of a false art historical unity, this exhibition not only liberates and drives a vital visibility to a wider array of depictions of performance, art and their publics but points out the path to correcting for a broken, myopic and too often money-obsessed system by abandoning it.

Darling Shear [36]

So where are you originally from?

! From Naperville. There's a stigma associated with Naperville. I don't know if it's a good or bad stigma, but I tell people I'm from Naperville and they're like, "Oh really? That explains a lot!" It's just a very wealthy town. They have two downtowns. It's really big, they have a lot of money over there. But then I moved to Atlanta when I was about 5 or 6 with my grandparents and my mother was just like, "I want you to have the suburban experience like I did." And, though we were living in the city at the time, "You're getting a little older and I want you to have a childhood like I did," because she didn't want me to be a city child.

I started dancing in the sixth grade and I started formal training as a Freshman at a performing arts high school, what's now called North Springs

36 Originally published at *Sixty Inches From Center*, Oct. 25, 2016, http://sixtyinches-fromcenter.org/movement-matters-darling-shear.

Charter School. Ballet, Modern, Jazz, African. It was very professional, as most schools are, but they prepped you so that if you were going to go into this profession, they gave you a lot of good tools.
They expected a lot of us.

I moved back to Chicago in 2011, I came back up to do some solo dancing. It was going good for a while and then I started doing burlesque, I did a lot of shows with Vaudezilla. I did that for a few years but still couldn't get into certain doors. So I was like, "I'll just do this until I get in somewhere. Then I came out as trans in October 2013, until then I was just queer and people didn't understand it, I guess? Non-conforming, just gender non-conforming. And I definitely had some obstacles because of that, I definitely — I'll just be very blunt: I'm a very likable person! I had a lot of friends, it was just a lot of the higher-ups, because they have been — I say this respectfully, but this is something we all face — they had been domesticated into going about a certain type of life and seeing things in a certain way and in the dance world if you're a woman you have to be a model woman and if you're a man you have to be a man and so, thankfully, contemporary dance has blurred those lines and made it a little more about the body instead of sexual identity. But I did bump heads with a few people just trying to move forward and get into certain doors because I was often looked at as a drag act. I would be at events or whatever, and people would just be like "Oh, are you the entertainment?" and I would just be like "…no, I'm one of your peers." So, it was a lot of that. But there were people who were always in my corner and invited me out to things and made sure I always had a ticket when I needed one, you know, to certain events. So, I just put my head down and moved forward, essentially.

Yeah. It does seem like there has been an important evolution, that there are so many more platforms out there.

Yeah the meeting we were just at [for Audience Architects] for the community convening, there were a number of different questions they were asking and one of them was about the number of gender-nonconforming trans dancers in attendance. And I was just like, "That wasn't even a question a few years ago." So, I'm happy the shift is happening but it was definitely rough and I didn't know what to do. Keep on dancing? Go into another field? It was very trying but I just kept working with people and it was funny, I was looking at my bio for a performance a few days ago and was like, "…has worked with Hinton Battle who played the scarecrow on The Wiz from the Broadway Production, two different soloists from Hubbard Street and soloists with Twyla Tharp, a Tracy Vogt with Philadanco, and I'm like, "What?! Shit is cray!" So why am I not getting into places?

Yes, and that was my next question: where you see
your work going and what you want to do?

> I think because I felt like such an outcast, I lost
> sight of what I wanted to do and went into night-
> life. And its been lovely. It's been good to me, and
> I have so many beautiful friends from it. But that's
> not where I wanted to be and so I did have to
> take time to step back and reexamine where I
> was going. Right now, I'm in the process of very
> actively doing more choreography and putting my
> work on other people. For the most part I am a
> soloist and I do love it but I have been getting
> more requests to set choreography for people. I've
> worked with Cerqua Rivera, with Jason Hancock
> for some future projects. I've done a lot of stuff
> for Erin Kilmurray. I'm a social butterfly. You have
> to get around, but it happens where you don't in
> Chicago because each part of town is like it's own
> little village. Right now I'm in Logan.

What would you like to see moving forward with the
trans and queer communities and how they develop
from where they're at now?

> I was thinking about this and for me, it's lovely
> to be the first something, but also awkward when
> you're the first. Whoopie Goldberg was saying a
> few months ago, she said, "Often when you're the
> first, you're forgotten about." It's like, what are your
> intentions for it, why are you doing it? And then

the other things is, whenever it's not a caucasian person that has done or created something, then it becomes about, "Oh, this black or, oh this trans, this gay," and it's like, "Yes, that's an aspect of it but that's not my everyday thing." Then when you are being highlighted for things that are about that, then it's in the proper platform and it's great and I acknowledge that, but it's not like I'm walking down the street with a sign on. It's in the list of things, but it's not the only thing. So, more recognition in general, but also to step away from this outer shell and really focus on what people are creating. I can only speak to the personal experience, but I've had some awesome moments through performance, where people came up to me and just saw a being, not all this other stuff. And that's what I look at creating with my performance, is to get people to feel something, see another person and not care about x, y and z. Only the message of we need to stop being so negative or be more open-minded. It is a lot to take that on.

Right, so your work is about period pieces. Evoking these ideals of femininity throughout different eras.

Yes, that's half of it. Half of it is historical jazz re-staging and re-enactments from film and television from the 20's up through about the 70's. And that came about working with Laurie Stallings, a performer and Hubbard Street dancer, who I also think dances for River Street North, working

with her in Atlanta and her company Glow ATL.
And we were doing a show called *Hinterland* and
Big Boi of Outkast, it was his album *Sir Lus-
cious Left Foot: The Son of Chico Dusty* had just
come out and so it was a free concert, and this
dance performance crazy foolishness — and about
20,000 people came out to this event, a parade
essentially that started out in a park and turned
into a procession and led to another space for the
after-party. So he had this one song called Gen-
eral Patton and I was in love with the song. I was
like, "What is the track that he sampled for the
song?" This was back in 2010. So finally after 3
days of research, I came across this one music blog
and they said he sampled the drum march from
Aida. So, a bell went off and I decided I wanted to
do something with this, because there's so much
stuff where people sample things from the past and
then these next generations think it's some new
song and it's like, "No, that actually came from this
person." Beyonce's *Crazy In Love* came from a
song I think by the Chi-Lites, and that song came
out in the '70s, so it's so much stuff where it has
been re-used and we think it's new.

So when you're presenting these, you're trying to
retain or reinstate some of the original context.

Some of them are reinterpretations because they're
big, choral pieces that has an ensemble and there's
these other things and I'm like, "I'm only a person

who can do so much." I wish I had the powers to multiply myself. But that's why I say restagings and re-enactments. It's not always step for step, but you get the gist of it, essentially. I spend a lot of time doing research, looking at videos, finding costumes, trying to get on the mark as possible. And a lot of the times too with video, certain camera angles and things there's only so much you can do, so just being realistic about it. So, I have that platform as an educational tool to inform people about who we are and where we come from and that's how a lot of people know me, through those works. Then I also do my contemporary works which are done — and I'll probably get in trouble with someone for saying this, but this is what it is and what I learned — using [Ohad Naharin's] Gaga technique. That's been interesting, because I usually am a person who is very neutral. I've basically said a lot of times I am basically Switzerland in a lot of political affairs. I wasn't raised dealing with politics in a lot of what's going on. Being a person with a voice that is heard by many now, it's very interesting navigating that. So, I'm very mindful about presentation and what I put out there. For the longest time there was an ongoing joke that I was a waspy white woman because I had a certain reserve about how I handle things. Because I do understand that people see something and form an opinion. Being that I am a trans woman of color, this is a fact. This is a thing that most people will only see and a lot of stigma comes with that. A lot of misinformation comes with that. So I work very hard to shift their view. And it is who I am — it is slightly exaggerated, but not that far off; it's probably about 20% more exaggerated than who I really am, since high school, basically. I've always been aware that people are watching, there's always a camera out there and this was before camera phones were really a thing, but I've always just been aware that cameras are out there and you have to watch your step. Thankfully, my grandfather is a music producer and DJ, he's been in the music industry since he was 16, and I've been blessed to meet some of the great names that a lot of people have grown up with and are now starting to introduce their children to. So, you learn things having conversations with them. I've also had some great mentors, there's a person who lives here named Erica Allen, she is the Chicago operations for Growing Power, which is an urban farming company. And then there's another woman by the name of Carol Kosciosko McCollom, she's a former model and stylist and public speaker who just does a lot of really great things to empower women. There's just so many, I couldn't begin to list all the people. Thankfully, I've had a lot of very strong women who helped me.

One of the first things I saw you in was the SWOP fundraiser. Is sex work a cause you've been involved in supporting for a long time or was it more of a one-off?

Yes, I have quite a few friends who do it. Again, it's just that stigma. It's just one of those things where like…so many people in government do it, who get caught with their pants down and try to turn around and wag their finger. It's just like, "But you were just…m'kay. Alright." And I think that was the thing for me, I was always supportive of it but I was very much definitely much more reserved and backed away from it, just because I was always nervous because…I don't want to be associated with this because I'm a trans woman and then that's already a thing that people associated with trans women and so it's just this whole thing. Then I finally got to the point where I was just, "I don't care anymore, you're going to think what you think, I know who I am." I love my friends. I want them to do whatever makes them happy, and sometimes you hustle. I don't hustle, personally. I do a Foxtrot or a quick step, but to each their own.

But yeah, everybody has to make ends meet.

Right, yes. And of course poverty can play a huge role, and people with fewer options are forced to turn to street economies to support themselves. It's not always optional.

Very true. I'll support that in any way that I can and so I started to create these pieces that are more sex-positive and sex worker positive. One piece I've been doing recently is Love For Sale, Ella Fitzgerald's version and it's very well received.

I think when you look at our history across the board, in many different societies and cultures, there's a certain platform we put sex workers on. There's this idea of this rags to riches thing, *Pretty Woman, Moulon Rouge*, there's so many different examples where as a culture we glorify it but at the same time wag our finger at it. I never pointed my finger because I've had a lot of fingers pointed at me, so I try to stay away from doing that but also I've had my moments where I wasn't in alignment with some of the things that were going on and it just took me some personal growth to look at the bigger picture.

Laurie Anderson ³⁷

Language of the Future premiered in 1984. It's an
amorphous, living changing performance that in
many ways mimics language and responds to changes
in the world. What compelled you to bring it to
Chicago and the Old Town School?

> Well, this is a work in progress and I'm always
> changing it a lot. So, it just has an old title but it's
> a lot of things about what's going on now polit-
> ically, it's kind of a template for things that are
> happening and I change it every day.

So, it's a surprise then even for you and will be
improvised in parts.

> I just finished a book for Rizzoli called *All the
> Things That I Lost in the Flood* and it's a bunch
> of stories, maybe we'll include some of those, we'll
> see what happens. I might include some things

37   Originally published in the *Chicago Tribune*, May 3, 2107.

from the past, I might include some things that I'm just improvising at the moment. We'll see. It's a kind of catchall but I'm going to bring along some images so there will be some animations I'm projecting and of course a lot of violin stuff, filters and things like that. But the reason I want to do that there is I really love small clubs. I really learned so much about what I'm doing because I'm able to see the audience and it's really a lot of fun for me. I'm looking forward to doing it there.

Yes, and Old Town has such a great music history, carrying on this rich tradition of folk music.

Right. Yes, it's really cool. And it's my hometown so it's always fun to be there to see relatives and friends. It's really cool — and Ken Nordine, who's one of my favorite people in the world. Oh gosh, maybe I'll call and see if he can come sit in. Maybe I shouldn't mention that since I didn't mention seeing him yet. So, never mind. But anyway, I love Ken so whenever I'm in Chicago I look him up.

So many of the formative experiences you've referred to throughout the years — the correspondence you had with JFK while you were running for student council and he was running for president, or the accident where you broke your back and were hospitalized — took place during your childhood in Glen Ellyn. And I wonder how much of the avant garde sensibility that flourished in the Midwest, outside

the commercial bubbles of the coasts, has informed
your work?

> I think what did influence it was using everyday
> stuff. I don't wear anything different for shows,
> I don't particularly talk differently than I would
> when I'm talking with you right now. It's not
> this rarefied thing, it really does come from this
> tradition of where people talk to — well, when
> I grew up there was also kind of a lot of weird
> stuff going on. I went to bible school as a kid and
> adults thought nothing of talking about snakes
> that could speak, oceans that would become dry in
> the middle and people coming back from the dead
> and I thought "Whoa! Adults are absolutely out of
> their minds!" Bible stories made a big, big impres-
> sion on me and I hadn't really realized how much
> until I was finishing this book and looking at how
> very much I've been attracted to how beautiful the
> language of the bible is. Especially Isaiah, it's really,
> really beautiful, wild poetry. I got into it even as a
> kid, that it was this other world of books. Plus, I
> really loved books as a kid and they came into my
> work in ways that I didn't even realize at the time,
> that I was making stuff. Not that I'm making this
> kind of retrospective book, I'm realizing a lot of
> influences that I didn't know I had.

There definitely exists this form of Midwestern mys-
ticism going back, that comes out of this sort of
Bible Belt influence and strains of Dixie revivalism
in response to the Great Migration.

Did you say "mysticism?"

Yes, mysticism.

Yeah! Yeah, I would agree with that, mysticism is a really good way to describe that because it's a fascination with these really wild tales!

Yes, this fascination with how to bring the imagination into the everyday and preserve this sense of illusion. At the expense of clarity.

Yep...

Speaking of — the opposite of that impulse, to me your techie, gearhead sensibility — has always seemed rooted in the swift ascendancy of computing technology in the '80s. And you've mentioned this "getting over the hump" of adapting to that new technology. What does that mean for how your work has and will change artistically and in terms of how you use technology?

I don't know if you ever really get over the hump, because it keeps shifting so fast and you really have to try to not let it drive you absolutely out of your mind because it really is escalating much more than in the '80s. Now, everybody is a multimedia artist, whether you call yourself that or not, you're working with all of this technology all the time — cameras and sound, and that wasn't the case then. And a lot of people use it well and some are just

drowning in it. It's just too much, they start real-
izing they can't have their Twitter and their emails
and their Facebook, they can't keep up with all of
that and I'm one of those people. I just — you
know, this morning I have about 50 appointments
in various media (laughs) it's really, really awful. It
convinces you that you can do more than you really
can because it's so fast and then you can't really
do all that stuff that you said. That's pretty much
where I am right now, I'm trying to finish up a big
virtual reality project for a big museum opening at
Mass MoCA in May and that's a huge project I've
been working on for a couple of years with a team
in Taiwan so I'm doing a lot audio and mixing for
that and tweaking the VR stuff. But VR for me is
an absolute dream because it means you can fly,
and it's really exhilarating. You know, initially we
used it as a kind of gaming medium but we get to
use it to build these whole, giant complexes that
are just made of words and it is just — I can really
get lost in it.

Yes, VR environments are actually pegged to our
real-world physics, so we use them simultaneously
for games and for modeling, say, the aerospace engi-
neering of a Mars landing.

In Chicago, I'm going to bring one little soft-
ware word thing that I have and it's something
I devised for the Kronos Quartet, it's something
I made for them. They said, "You know, we want

to tell stories with our instruments," and I said, "Well, how about you play? You're really good at playing, you don't need to really tell stories," and then I said "well, I can invent some software so you can tell stories with your instruments." They said, "Great!" And I realized I don't know how to do that. So, anyway, I'm going to bring to Chicago one of the programs that I made for that and show how it works.

I read you recently described your husband's life as a process of "entering into ancestry." What does that mean for you, how you see where you and your work are today and the place you're interested in establishing?

I can't remember saying that. "Entering into ancestry?" What does that mean? I don't know, really, because I'm so much more interested in the future than the past so my husband, Lou (Reed), he had so many beautiful songs and did so many amazing things and I feel like I have a lot of access to all of that. And also, we've been working with this archive a long time so I feel very, very close to him although he's been dead almost 4 years. And there will be a couple of songs dedicated to him in Chicago, and a sort of weird duet as well.

Last one: how's the new puppy you got after Lola-belle passed, Little Will?

He doesn't play the piano, he doesn't do anything.
He loves to eat and goof around. He's a great dog,
he's really really good. Having a blast.

J'Sun Howard [38]

You don't hail originally from Chicago, correct?

No, I'm originally from Chattanooga, TN. I came here in 2001 to go to school at Columbia College. Here, I started out on the West Side. Then to Lakeview, which was fun, crazy, and full of self-discovery. Uptown was chill and where I began to feel more grounded. I went back to Lakeview after that, and by twenty-three I was done with the bar/club scene. South West Side in the 'hood, around the Homan Square area was next, I would carry a small blade in my mouth in case I had to defend myself. It wasn't the safest place I've lived. I got Humboldt Park but I didn't feel like home after my two closest friends, Margaret Morris and Angela Gronroos, left. Now that I'm in Pilsen, I wish I'd lived here all along. I don't think I would've struggled so much with how much rent is here. But I feel like I need a break from Chicago

38   Originally published at *Sixty Inches From Center*, April 27, 2017, http://sixtyinches-fromcenter.org/movement-matters-jsun-howard.

and to spend a couple of years elsewhere. I've been thinking about cities like Oakland, Portland, New York City, Philadelphia, Berlin, Lyon, Kobe, or Tokyo. Maybe I'll do graduate studies in one of these places after I finish my undergraduate degree at the School of the Art Institute.

Where does the interest in dance come from for you?

Well, growing up I was never like, "I want to be a ballet dancer," or anything like that. I was one of the kids who would record and watch the '90s Hip Hop and R&B videos to learn the choreography in them, like Janet Jackson, Michael Jackson, Missy Elliott, Aaliyah … I knew there were people who do choreography but didn't think or research it as a viable career. At the time, I was interested in being a biochemist or an accountant. I know, strange options, but I think those things still are active in my creative work somehow. My senior year in high school is when I decided to abandon the normative, cyclical 9-5 system and actually follow a dream to be an artist, i.e. a poet. I was more comfortable with words than with this idea of my body having words then. When our high school, City High, switched to a magnet arts one, Center for the Creative Arts, I chose Creative Writing as my focus although I did participate in the dance/step team. I wouldn't say I was afraid of being in the dance program; I didn't know where to begin. I guess I could've asked but it all seemed a little too late. During an award ceremony my senior year of high school, just after I received the last of three, this one for creative writing, I chose dance. The decision was abrupt and it was right.

Who would you say were the biggest influences or mentors in terms of the work you make now?

The only Hip Hop choreographer I say inspired me was Fatima Robinson — highly underrated. Many of the '90s Hip Hop and R&B videos were choreographed by her. Her playful yet sensual nuances, idiosyncratic rhythmic choices, and the embodiment of narrative in her work were able to guide me in dreamscapes with these music videos. In that regard, I try to make dreamscapes with my choreographic work too. In order to get somewhere, you have to dream. Otherwise, what's the point? I didn't have a mentor in high school or the three two and a half years I was at Columbia College. I do wonder how my journey would've changed if I had. To see a black male be a poet or choreographer and learn from them would've been an asset and miraculous to my artistic growth. Bill T. Jones was an inspiration, but by the time I met him or went to take one of the intensives, I had already decided to not dance in a company. I knew I wasn't that kind of dancer. When Jones's company visited the Dance Center in 2003, I asked him about mentoring me but he disclosed an unfortunate experience he had mentoring someone and decided that he wouldn't do it any-more. In the dance department at Columbia, I'd say Krenly Guzman was the dance teacher I gravitated towards the most. I took his class every semester. The quality, sophistication, poeticism, and lushness of his movement style captivated me. My goal was to transmute all of that in/onto my body. Of course, I'm still working at it. Spirals seem to get away from me. During this time, I didn't know the kinds of work I wanted to make. They were experiments to uncover what's in my voice. I'm a quiet person and also wanted to see what waited/waits behind that. For Student Per-formance Night at the Dance Center, one piece I did called *transmigration: a suffusing coalescing flight*. I think it was the only successful choreo-graphic project I did during my time at Columbia because it felt like I was finally opening. And flight is a theme I continue to go back to, exploit, sub-vert, and re-imagine. Today, he probably doesn't agree with me, but Darrell Jones is my mentor. I don't know how to attest to how much depth, rigor, and sublimity has permeated my work from our movement research and collaborations.

That's great, it's true. Dreams are so essential to that pro-cess. Where do you think you and your work are today?

Where am I at today? Hmmm, well, the solo I put on Damon Green and the piece I'm about to make through Links Hall's SET FREE residency this year can be compartmentalized in Queer Blq Futur Narratives. But the cartography of everything I'm doing falls under what I call "poetic testimonies." How I (or we) bear witness to the troubles and brokenness of this dimension. I don't think I'll stray from making poetic testimonies. But the challenge will be making them, or iterations of them, that are impactful, touching, and speak to the current times to come. I'm interested the idea of the future because it can reveal what it means to survive and evolve. Even though there are a lot of visual artists now like Nick Cave, Krista Franklin, Hebru Brantley, and Rashid Johnson working in AfroFuturism, I want to see how it can transmute into a choreographic lens specifically from a person of color's viewpoint. I don't call myself a visual artist but I drew this self-portrait as an Anime character and have been thinking how being a monster (as the media has portrayed black men to be) is a modality of survival. And why do I always have to be strong? On the flipside of that, I've been thinking about joy and how to use it to make dreamscapes that are charismatic and euphoric. (I know, an enigmatic dichotomy). Joy is important to seek out these days, knowing where our country is going. It's a form of resistance. So why become a wounded bird that'll land on anything? Moving forward, I want to devise work that creates new paradigms in which queer people of color not only survive but thrive and become magical birds. These landscapes aren't going to be constructed for us, so seeing them performed can give folks perspective doing it in their real lives.

Damon Green performing *Working on Better Versions of Prayers*.
Image by Stephanie Toland.

Is it important then for you to try and move towards innovation in your work, or do you see it as relying on, say, poetic traditions?

I try to not think that I'm innovating, which may be a way to be innovative. I trust that whatever I'm making has the merit to stand on its own. Since I'm a rare black unicorn in the dance community, I try to make things that a rare black unicorn would. I don't know if this is a game or (again) a survival tactic, but I try to not think like everyone else and push myself to be unique and fuel my curiosity to be at the edge of something. When I think about artists who are my contemporaries, I can count them on one hand in Chicago, which is quite problematic. It doesn't bring me to the forefront either. It's as if there's enough room in the garden for a flower to bloom in the shaded area no one really wants to take notice of. When I look beyond this city, artists in NYC like Ni'ja Whitson, niv Acosta, NIC Kay, Rashaad Newsome, Brother(hood) Dance! (Ricarrdo Valentine and Orlando Hunter), Niall Niall, Jonathan Gonzalez, and many more are all fabricating these constellations I see my work in relation.

In terms of what you've accomplished in your work so far, what do you see as having been the most successful?

To date, my most successful artistic aspiration was being selected for the Chicago Dancemaker's Lab Artist Award in 2014. It was affirming, especially as an emerging artist. I applied on a whim. At the time, only my close friends knew I was ready to quit this artistic journey. I was ready to delete my social media accounts, change my phone number, go back to Chattanooga, and start completely over. I was fed up with seeing work that was uninspiring or a complete waste of time/effort, I got rejected from everything I applied for up until then, and any work that I found wasn't worth the hustle. I don't know which diviner decided to cast a string of gold my way just enough, but I'm still here. In that sense, what has worked has been forging forward and trusting my creative work will lead me to places I've never dreamed of going. Patience is vital. But sometimes patience feels like a con. So I started reaching out to people I wanted to collaborate and/or work with. I asked Thomas DeFrantz if I could do a residency at Duke University, and in 2018 I'm going there to work in the SLIPPAGE laboratories for a couple of weeks. I stopped waiting for rejections (they still invade my inbox though) and discover ways to make it happen on my own and with the help of admirers of my work. I do have goals like becoming a Princeton Fellow, doing a Lannan Residency, winning a Bessie Award for Choreography, a Doris Duke Artists Award, and an Alpert Award, or just being commissioned for the Lyon Opera Ballet to name a few, but I know I'll get these one day. I often wonder how my artistic career would be different if I had a BFA and MFA, but I can check back in with you when I have them.

Where does identity fit into your work for you, if it does, and what's necessary to push back against a system that often unnecessarily problematizes depictions of the black or brown body in dance?

I kind of get irritated when I have to answer a question like this. I or people who look like me aren't the problem. I can say how a lot of the times, I feel like I'm a mouse being coaxed with just enough crumbs to be comfortable inside a labyrinth that supposedly has exits. There's all these panels, symposiums, think pieces, scholarly papers, and social media battles on how to dismantle white supremacy, but white people don't want to do the work that takes to dismantle it. Talking in circles, circles are labyrinths. So who's afraid of taking one for our team. Black bodies do it daily. To go against white supremacy, I do rituals that make me feel whole and connected to nature/others.

Dedrick Gray and W ll Harris performing *Working on Better Versions of Prayers.*
Image by Stephanie Toland.

From preparing a delicious home cooked meal, long walks, getting lost, staying up all night thinking about holy things, writing poetry and reading poets like Danez Smith, Jayy Dodd, Morgan Parker, Clint Smith, Paul Tran, Ocean Vuong, Kaveh Akber, Hanif Willis-Abdurraqib, Roger Reeves, listening to podcasts like The Read, 2 Dope Queens, the Friend Zone, PostBourgie, Helga, Ignorant Philosophy, laugh at myself, watching my niece Chloe grow up, traveling, making sure I give hugs and tell people close to me I love them and so on and so on. To go against white supremacy, I have to live how it doesn't want me to live.

What I think dancemakers of color should start doing is creating institutions for investigation and incubation. Even though Theaster Gates receives criticism for the work he's doing on the South Side, he's an example to follow. I'm going to apply for the ArtPlace National Creative Placemaking Fund because it would be significant and crucial for Pilsen to have a space dedicated to movement research, choreographic inquiry and performance alongside the many art galleries here. "Placekeeping" can be a way to combat the gentrification that's occurring in Pilsen. Plus, this space can be curated in a fashion that can reinvent and change the current model to promote dancemakers of color better than other institutions have. In addition, organizations and non-for-profits around

Chicago should analyze data from the past eight to ten years to see if their programming was diverse, equitable. I can tell you from experience that most aren't. For us, by us is imperative if we want to see change. I hope Damon Green's dance studio, TextureDance, is successful and becomes influential in Chicago's dance community.

And then there's education, and how the economics of it is violence towards people of color. Many people of color decide not to pursue an art degree because there isn't money in it. And in order to contest the economic violence, you need a salary that will uproot you from the stagnation the system causes. I know some younger folk who don't want to go to college because they're afraid of having "good" debt. Most artists making their way through the dance/performance world go through this step by step acquisition of merit from one award/grant/residency to the next. And within this structure, it hardly ever recognizes artists who have not acquired an MFA degree. Yesterday, on Facebook an organization I follow for scholarship opportunities posted Milo Yiannopoulos has a white privilege scholarship for white male undergraduates. I could only laugh, and hope it was a joke. Many dance departments at college and universities should have full rides, fellowships, and emergency funds to ensure their students not only reach their potential but surpass it. Retention of students is a major problem for art schools, but

> I still don't see anything being done to remedy it. Returning to SAIC, knowing that admitted students get merit scholarships, would mine increase since I've received more merits? People think art is an easy thing to do but it's only easy when you don't have to worry about living.

Those are all important insights. Thanks so much for
taking the time to have this conversation with me.
Any last thoughts before we wrap up?

> Promoting and curating queer emerging artists of color is becoming more immediate in my artistic practice because of the lack of programming I see around the city. And it helps equip the generation after me to do better than I did.

Thanks, J'Sun. Very much looking forward to seeing
that work!

Allen Moore [39]

You're coming out of a multidisciplinary background, working in visual art and DJ'ing, and recently you've been working a lot with Comfort Station in Logan Square.

> Yea. I got in touch with Jordan Martins in early fall. They were looking for a group of people to not only curate, but to volunteer. I applied, talked to Jordan, and a group of us got together and started doing it. It's been a really fun time. We've been slated to curate throughout 2017. We just had a show called *Gather* and we'll all have some of our work there, too. We're really focusing on how to make [Comfort Station] into a very open space. We're still discussing it. We know that we really want it to be political, especially right now, but at the same time not be too heavy. We don't want to hit anybody over the head.

39   Originally published at *Sixty Inches From Center*, Jan. 9, 2017, http://sixtyinches-fromcenter.org/movement-matters-allen-moore.

> For me, as an African American [artist], [politics have] completely influenced my work. And at Comfort Station, we want to have it open to [everyone]. We just had a workshop for making protest banners–I got to make one. I grew up in Robbins, Illinois, which is a small black town. There weren't a lot of expectations for me coming up through that. Now, fast forward and think about Donald Trump becoming President —

I don't even want to think about it.

> I don't want to think about it either. It's like night and day but…having to try, as an African American, to navigate bodies of work that talk about [the election] as organically as possible and also navigate my own [interests]. Not to say it's [only] my own interests, but sometimes it flows together and we [feel a] responsibility of, "Oh, I have to do this." I think we're facing that at Comfort Station. We're thinking about that [responsibility].

Yes, and Comfort Station is in this communitarian tradition of domestic or alt-spaces in Chicago where you can perhaps present more politically-charged work whereas more commercial spaces might shy away from it because it's bad for business.

> Exactly. I think the way we've come into it has been a good thing. We [recognize that we] should talk about the social and political stuff and the rights of

individual people. We had our first show not to test the waters, but just to get it down. We don't know if we're going to stick with the title of the series, Gather. But we might. We just want to keep trying to find performers and cross-sections of art from sound, visual, and all sorts of things that show the conversation. We want to encourage people to [see Comfort Station as] a place where people can talk and be honest about what's going on.

Right. It's a climate where a lot of the people who are taking power are clearly bigoted, and are creating this environment of encouragement for people to act that way too.

Encouragement, entitlement …

Right now, my money comes from working in Glen Ellyn, Illinois. I'm a manager at a wine and sip place called Bottle and Bottega—as horrible as it sounds. There, I'm dealing with various entitled people — whom are everywhere. But I remember the night that Trump won. There was a party in where I work and I was like, "Yep, that's exactly right." And it's just interesting the words that you hear. I had a woman come in who was friends with the owner and talking about African Americans — first of all, she was working for a non-profit to help kids from the inner-cities, which is great, but with the way that she framed it, somehow the conversation went to black fatherhood and how we, [black people], do it to ourselves.

What? It infuriates me that people dismiss how
much language actually matters. She might have
just have said "those people."

She probably did. But then I had to sit there and
serve this person.

That's demoralizing. So, *Gather* is about getting
people together in the same place to talk and discuss
these kinds of experiences.

Exactly. In the same place and where we can feel
comfortable. We want to grab [inspiration] from
experimental sound; I think everybody else in the
curatorial group is all music, though I also have
a Master's in painting. The last [Gather] more
painting and sound. I'm not going to lie, I'm not
exactly — I don't want to say trained — but I'm
more of a 2-D person who organically found a
way to incorporate my love of music [into my art].

They're all art forms.

Yes, exactly. That's my philosophy. And I think
that's all of our philosophies. We are looking at
experimental sound, we are looking at something
that might not necessarily have other venues [to
house them]. We want to bring in people and the-
matically make sure we go over the intersections

how the [themes are] all going to meet. We dis-
cussed shows that might [include] completely
different practices or things like that. It's inter-
esting. There's already a lot of representation of
things like 2-D work in galleries and I think when
Jordan brought it to us, he was very for Comfort
Station being used as a space [for sound] because
of its awesome acoustics. But also, we thought it
would be a nice thing for people in the community
to come see. So, that's how we got on the track
of having this be more of a performance space. I
think it's a good place for people. And you kind of
have to be up front–and that's what we want. We
want it to be a place where people can perform, but
also where people in the community who are just
walking past can come to see something that they
won't otherwise see on a Friday or Saturday night.
I mean, there's a lot of shit to go and see out there.

Right, so this becomes a little island of creativity in
a sea of commercial options out there.

That's right. And if you don't mind, I might just
steal that one.

Hah! It's yours, take it. So this push for a political
context, is that in response to a sense that there's
this revanchist potential for return to erasure? Of
the dialogue getting watered back down?

> Yes — I think it's all that. But it's important to us that we come to it as organically as possible. I think in the current climate, all the things leading up to Donald Trump becoming president–you can't avoid it. If you [tried], it wouldn't work. And that would make it not as unique as we want to it be. But there are a lot of places and a lot of galleries that would be afraid —

Right, it would hurt business.

> Right. And the only profit we want is profit for artists. You know, people give donations. Then, too, we've put together documentation for the work [for the artists]. And we've had people perform who may not be able to get documentation for the work. That's something we can give the performers. We can offer that. So, we want not only to have this relationship with the community, we not only want to be honest and talk about a lot of the social and political issues, but we also [want to] create a venue where the artists can come, bare their souls and get something from it. With the donations, we just split it evenly and don't take anything from it. I think that's how Comfort Station has been, but we're looking out now for more grants and that kind of thing.

What has personally drawn you to this work? It's your politics, of course.

Yes. And also coming up African American in Robbins, Illinois, which I won't get into. But it's also my adopted attitude about people. I love working with people, even though we all suck at different times. But I do like people–artists especially. Coming into this I want to be able to be there and help people, but I also want to be a [positive] representation. Like I said about the music scene, I think back to that conversation with one woman that really sticks out. She said, "Oh, well people who are very talented and living in the city are still not the same as those who can work with formal composition." I want to fight against that. I don't believe that being prim and proper is necessary or the formal representation of music, sound, and art. I want to, hopefully, be a representation of that [expanded view]. I'm learning a lot in addition to what we're putting out there. I'm also making a lot of relationships, which is something you want to do in any art form. You want to network. And if I can help build a venue for people, for performers and especially for people of color, that's it.

And performance within the Western canon has been such a white person's field. Especially dance, but also performance art. And that's clearly a problem.

Yes. People of color are kind of funneled. I know I was funneled. Growing up African American, I was funneled either into football, rap, or some other sport. That's what I think is a consensus for a lot of people. But there is so much more in life, so much more in art and, yes, there has been an over-representation of white — and definitely an under-representation of people of color. I know I'm the only person of color in the curatorial group, but we've had an open dialogue and think we've all come to that naturally. We want to open it and make it more inclusive of people of color, but we want to come to that organically. We want to open it up for all people and not be exclusionary in any way. The work that we look for and the type of experimental sound that we like has just worked out so far.

And has that been influenced by your work at places like Experimental Sound Studios (ESS)? I know they've gone through a transition recently losing their founder.

Yes! Lou Mallozzi. I had put in a proposal with them. I had the pleasure of meeting Lou and having him critique my work about a year and a half ago at ACRE. That was a really great experience. I got the chance to communicate and talk with him. Then, my first major performance within that form was at ESS. Before that, I was in Dekalb at NIU, so I did a lot of my work there. I had a studio there and the transition for me was sculptural. I was experimenting with everything, so when I started doing sound, it opened up this gigantic world and I didn't know but as I was

moving through it step by step. I was in a space
of sound. It is the most natural thing for me and
my work.

I knew that ESS was where I wanted to go, and I
was very lucky to get accepted. The performance
was amazing. I totally intend to record there
more—as often as possible.

Growing up as kid, there was a time when my
mom got very, very sick and had experimental
surgery. She almost died. It was a very rare dis-
ease. She's where the music comes from–my love
of sound and the work with the graphite records.
When I started drawing as a kid, I drew from
record covers and record labels. I would just sit
there and look at the typography of speakers
because my mom had a nice Fischer receiver and
record player. I'd sit and draw George Michael
or *Wham!* album covers. A lot of artists [learn
that way]. They don't know what they're doing and
they don't get a lot of direction. I didn't get shit
from high school. For a while I had no clue about
grad school or anything like that, but I was lucky
enough to gravitate toward the right places and
people. And that's what we hope the conversations
we're hosting will be.

Bebe Miller [40]

Your last visit to Chicago was in 2012, the improvisation festival at the old Links Hall. What about the aMID Festival do you find compelling enough to return?

I was interested in performing with these other dancers. We're all in the same program, I respect them, so there was that and most of my company performances involve other dancers at this point in our work. And I have done a bunch of performing on my own in recent years, so I thought, "Hm! This is worth pursuing. So I'll perform an improvisational solo and duet. I'm working with Darrell Jones, with whom I have a long history and I kind of thought I'd see where the two of us are. I think my thoughts about performing at this point in my career and in my dancing life, a lot of it is, "Where am I now? Why is this interesting and who am I with?" So that is the nature of our

40   Originally published at *Occasional Inquiries,* Jan. 25, 2016, https://medium.com/occasional-inquiries/all-told-bebe-miller-the-gift-of-the-present-moment-bf85a98daa52.

exploration and the nature of mine that I do on my own as well. So I asked Darrell if he'd be interested in participating and we don't know what that will be, but we're both open to it. I'm also doing another improvisation with other members of the Bebe Miller Company as the year is progressing, so I feel as though I'm entering into a series of performances in some way.

How do you think all of that informs the moment we're living now, with the #blacklivesmatter movement? How much do these social advancements inform your work?

Well, I think it's informing my life. I don't feel that I'm making a different statement about an African American woman living in our times. I think our times are inescapable. What I do feel, maybe not so much in the last couple of years, but this is over a generation and what has become clear is we are more taken for granted in the range of stories or what have you in relation to our personal identities that are out there. Back in my early days there was an expectation that there was a black story that needed to be told and I think we moved through to an understanding that they all need told, and it's not just the black ones. But I think that our political reality, if you have your eyes open, is that there's an inescapable, and it shouldn't be escaped. I don't think I need to say that this dance is about #blacklivesmatter, this is a black life that matters on its own.

In relationship to that question, especially when it comes to dance, is distinctly ageist and defined by a populist youth cult.

It's not just America, but the field of dance is considered a young person's thing. I'm in my 60's, we know that it's not just a young person's field anymore and — all hats off to aMID for doing this — but I think it's even beyond that. I think we're living, in the field, a moment where artists of my generation, there is more an expectation and evidence that we just keep on going, whether we're writing or filmmaking or doing more spoken word, performing or choreographing. I think that there is more and more evidence, of my generation's time, of this sense that we are still here. I've also been doing this series of performances with the Wooster Group in New York called *Early Shaker Spirituals*, and they're a group of 5 women and we are all pretty much 60 and over, including Frances McDormand, Suzzy Roche, Cynthia Hedstrom — I mean Frances McDormand is recognizable in one field, but you know, we're all of a certain age and we're singing these Shaker songs. So, for me, just the fact of my age as a performer isn't so much an issue. Matter of fact, I feel it's getting well-used. There was also the *5 First Ladies of Dance*, a reminder of the series we toured until 2010 that was Carmen de Lavallade, me, Jawole Willa Jo Zollar, Germaine Acogny and Dianne McIntyre, so African American women of a certain age. I was the young one! So, this isn't the first one, and I feel that maybe we are in a time when we can relax a bit and just let us do what we do, because it's seen as valuable and there's something to say without just saying that we're older. So, one would hope.

Who are some of your favorite up-and-comers?

This is one of the hardest things about leaving New York is that I'm really more out of touch with emerging artists than I ever have been. I'm always interested in the work that Darrell is doing, and Angie Hauser. I feel like I'm watching closer to my generation these days; Tere O'Connor, Cynthia Oliver than the young and up-and-coming. Unfortunately, I'm not in that audience because it's not happening so much.

What do you want the audience to take away for this event?

I hope that Darrell and I are able to create a particular atmosphere or a sense of place and time that captivates. I feel like — and maybe this is age speaking — but I feel like I'm really interested in being in the moment and that in and of itself is a gift to us as performers, but also when I'm watching something. I want to see how involved I can become, and just be with these people now. So, my biggest thing is just, can we connect? So, that's it.

Nic Kay [41]

How did you make your way to Chicago? You're originally from…

I was born in The Bronx. Though I grew up in between the Bronx, Brooklyn, and Manhattan, which was REAL. Not easy. Not romantic. Just simply very R A W. New York City is unforgiving, especially unforgiving if you or your parental guardians are working paycheck to paycheck, which is nearly 60 percent of the population currently. After I left home/was forced out at 17, I grew to understand this reality independently navigating the streets and drop-in/shelter programs in the city. I don't need to describe the culture and fashion and the club scene because those narratives are readily available in media. Chicago is where I came alive. As a teenager I was super inspired by Chicago's political organizing and experimental theater scene and wanted to be a part of the

41   Originally published at Sixty Inches From Center, March 17, 2017, http://sixty-inchesfromcenter.org/movement-matters-nic-kay.

movement. In 2011, I gathered my coins and moved from Brooklyn, New York to Chicago's North side to join a community of activists and artists who were building a world I wanted to live in. I worked at Apple on the Magnificent Mile, took classes at Columbia College, hung out at SAIC, and had a fellowship at About Face Youth Theatre. I was serious about the hustle, lol. I'm currently living between Chicago and New York City.

What drew you to dance?

Gestures — dance — movement were my first language. How I announced myself to the world. It has been how I've made sense of my changing body, my neighborhood, culture etc. The habitus developed into a conscious practice when I began experiencing severe depressive episodes at the age of 10. I began to somatically understand the power of movement and dance in letting it all out, dealing with the harshness of life. In 2010, I decided that art making and doing was going to be my career. I performed my first solo performance, Wonderful, during the exhibition Into The Neon at a Chashama space in New York. I was so nervous, but afterward there was no turning back. I was on a path.

What dancers inspired what you do with the art form? Were there particular mentors who nourished you along the way?

I had a babysitter who would take all of us kids after school to the New York Public Library in the Bronx. I discovered the biography of the prolific Katherine Dunham one day trolling the aisles. Ms. Dunham's practice of research into Caribbean dance and ethnography was eye opening to say the least. It was electric: the images of her twisting, moved by the music. It was a sort of spiritual experience that I could relate to because I was very often in the church. I hadn't seen any live footage until I was much older. I have also been very inspired by the videos of Missy Elliott and the work of the hip-hop director and choreographer Fatima Robinson. What I discovered about myself and my work, from my admiration of their practices, was that I desired above all to have the agency to determine the direction of my practice, research, and productions. Three quotes/statements that are currently on sticky notes on my desktop that are guiding my current explorations – Pina Bausch: "I do not care how people move, but what moves them." Paris is Burning: "You own everything." Revelations "came from [Alvin] Ailey's 'blood memories' of his childhood in rural Texas and the Baptist Church."

How would you describe the political exigency of the work you make today, and where do you think it's headed next?

The works I'm married to right now are all about gestures of resistance. My practice is about how to move when you are meant to disappear. My practice is located within a history of black, trans, radical, queer communities who have and continue to do/make art as a mode of understanding, celebration, and survival. I am a mover, deeply invested in the history of performance and the black body as performative. To make art and do art is a political and spiritual commitment for me. I am making to survive and develop a practice of appreciation, celebration, and mourning. Right now, I am working in between two projects: Cotton Dreams and Get Well Soon! Cotton is a transdisciplinary project (printmaking, bookmaking, collage, sound, video, and performance), which was birthed out of being gifted a bouquet of cotton by a white stranger in Soho, NYC. Get Well Soon! is a project based on a phrase indicating a hope of recovery. In summary, the following quote from Favianna Rodriguez best expresses my desires and intentions as an artist and active citizen: "Art is a path to freedom, emancipation, and equity. While many people proclaim to understand the power of art, I think few understand the role of art in challenging structures of systemic injustice — the power of art in transforming the imagination, and in building true, lasting social change."

How do you think your work innovates on the history of different kinds of approaches to dance and movement art making?

My work expands and innovates what has come before by not seeking the approval of white gate-keepers in the fields of art/performance/dance and not depending on these bodies for sole funding in order to build and share my practice. This is important because many artists' research and practices are shaped by what grants/fellow-ships/buyers are interested in seeing. Through utilizing the internet I have been able to grow audiences internationally who are interested in my blend of styles and study from other art-ists sharing videos and tutorials online. The true innovation is understanding that rules are to be broken and that any great movement in dance first looked to many as absolutely absurd.

What do you consider your most successful work, and why?

My most successful artistic aspiration was to write and perform my first full-length solo performance. And I did that in 2015 with the premiere of *lil BLK* at Links Hall in Chicago. *lil BLK* is an experimental solo performance influenced by New York City gay/queer ballroom culture, live punk shows, butoh, and praise dance. *lil BLK* is a story about a fairy boi, child of god, little black girl, per-former, and activist. The story plays out through a series of biographical moments that are equal parts narrative and dream. To date, I have performed the show about six times all over the world. I have learned that things take time. I wanted to have completed *lil BLK* in 2011. It took many years to bring the dream to actualization. I needed to grow as a mover and make the network possible to support my aspirations. Despite it being a solo performance, so many people are involved in making the show a success.

How do you respond to the white supremacy of not just the wider culture, but the structures it imposes on representation in dance and performance?

In 1981, Audre Lorde said in her talk "The Uses of Anger: Women Responding to Racism:" "My response to racism is anger. I have lived with that anger, ignoring it, feeding upon it, learning to use it before it laid my visions to waste, for most of my life. Once I did it in silence, afraid of the weight. My fear of anger taught me nothing. Your fear of that anger will teach you nothing, also." The biggest resistance I feel living in a white supremacist culture is problematizing my anger and the denial that we are actually all living in a white supremacist culture and that despite one's personal intentions to be a "good" person, you are either complicit in this or actively resisting this fact. My personal practice works to push back against this by being unapologetic and once again embodying the eloquent words of Lorde in *The Black Unicorn*, when she says, "So it is better to speak remembering we were never meant to survive."

Many things need to change, not just for black artist(s) but all artists who are othered and experience violence under the current order. If you are wondering what changes need to happen to make the system better for ALL artists, specifically in the United States — I would suggest these two readings: *On the Power of Art and Challenging Cultural Inequity in ART 21* by Favianna Rodriguez and *Act now!*, where Brittany Williams launches a challenge to arts leaders.

Aaron Hughes & Amber Ginsburg[42]

Thank you for taking the time to speak with me today. I take it, from your description of the *Tea Project*, that on some level it's about trying to focus the national conversation on our sense of collective trauma; do you feel like your experiences on tour in Iraq left you traumatized? And do you feel like our culture effectively responds to that, and in what way is that, or is it not related, to what you're doing with the *Tea Project*?

It's definitely all connected and related. I have a V.A. rating for post-traumatic stress disorder. I think, in a lot of ways, our whole society is dealing with different kinds of trauma from the fact that we've been at war for so long and, dealing with the structural violence of our society, and

42   Originally published at *Occasional Inquiries*, April 7, 2016, https://medium.com/occasional-inquiries/confronting-systemic-racism-the-global-war-on-terror-over-tea-f845128d1d42.

I'm interested in constructing this space that can connect those dots. Perhaps use some of the sensationalizing of veterans' trauma to deconstruct that narrative and reconnect to the notion that we're all struggling with these issues and living through these experiences. I hesitate to make this project or any project I'm involved with about therapy or directly about healing. I mean, I think healing is a very important thing that we all need. But we need survival as well, and I think a lot of times these terms "healing" and "therapy" and "trauma" tend to de-politicize situations that are extremely political. I think there's a lot of power dynamics involved that we're trying to negotiate in this project and acknowledge, and to acknowledge how we fail at dealing with them a lot of times. How I failed at dealing with a lot of the problematic structures of power through the military when I was deployed. That's even a part of why I never accepted tea while I was deployed. I didn't have tea with Iraqis or third-country nationals or Kuwaitis because we were told it was a security threat because we were told it could be poisoned and underneath all of that was really this racism and Islamophobia. I'm interested in holding a space to acknowledge how these situations arise, where people's fears get so built-up that they can't accept a cup of tea. And what is the reason to accept a cup of tea, and what does it mean to offer a cup of tea? What does it mean to these Iraqis who have lived through these occupations and lost a great deal of their

dignity and they still have this gesture of hospi-
tality? I know this is a long statement and maybe
not helpful —

No, it's extremely helpful.

— but it's just that at the end of Guantanamo Dia-
ries, Mohamedou [Ould Slahi's] lawyers comment
that even after this book that documents his torture,
his extra-legal detention, his extraordinary rendi-
tion first from Afghanistan and then later on to
Guantanamo, later on he says, "I wish and I hope
everyone who has been mentioned in this story and
in this narrative reads it and corrects any of the mis-
takes, that one day we can all sit down and have tea
together and talk about all that we've learned." And
to me, that's such a generous offer of hospitality from
someone who's lived through so much violence and
is still detained in Guantanamo.

Can I just add one thing to this? About this ques-
tion of trauma or however you want to frame it.
You know, working with Aaron, our dynamic is
really interesting because I'm in what is gener-
ally termed a "civilian" position, right? If you're a
veteran, the complement term to veteran would
be civilian, or citizen, or some other way of dif-
ferentiating from not having participated in the
military and the longer I'm in the project, the
longer I'm resisting that binary. I think we are all
as citizens and as veterans — and this term, I've

been trying to find language for which I'm now calling "non-veterans" — as a citizen and non-veteran, I'm deeply implicated and ever-involved in the state of war that we're in. And so, when we sit down and have tea, all of these things that are in place to separate our experiences through language and definition, those are the kinds of binary structures we hope can get dissolved in these kinds of moments, or work to get dissolved in these moments.

So, it's a sort of awareness of the military-cultural intersectionality that you're pursuing.

Yes. Exactly. Very well put.

I agree with you, and if this is to some degree pro-testation against those binaries and the systemic evidence of them, how much of it is social, how much of it is part of the cultural divides that you're encountering? I'm not sure that's something you can speak so much about outside of actually engaging in the performance, but I'm curious.

I think in some way it's up to others to determine — some people might call it protest art, some people might not — I feel like it narrates based off of perspective and relationship to the piece. I do think we are trying to push back on some of the overarching political and cultural narratives in our society and create a space for people to share how those dominant narratives affect us not only for veterans but especially for all the individuals that have been affected by these wars domestically. Whether it's the equipment that I never even had, or coming home to police departments in the United States or the fact that a lot of the targeting of Muslim, asian, black and brown communities that have been targeted overwhelmingly by our domestic and foreign policies, I think all these things, these wars don't necessarily just exist in some far-off land. They exist in the refugees that come here, they exist in the fact that right now, the NSA is collecting our cell phone data, you know?

So it's something we're all negotiating.

The other thing that I'd maybe resist — maybe not resist, but question — about this notion of protest art is how one of the things about the performances themselves, of offering tea and prompting questions from very personal stories, is how it elicits other people's personal stories. While this is a performance, it's also an invitation and there are very, very few spaces where we're good at holding disagreement. So it's not that the performance particularly advocates a given position, it's a way of talking about things that don't get talked about, so responses to these performances — who's there? The politics of the people who are there isn't wholly pre-determined. It might be partially pre-determined by certain proclivities, but it's not wholly pre-determined so it's not clear that everyone in the audience is against the Iraq war or against these other things. If we took a stand of a protest position directly, that eliminates the possibility for contradictory voices to exist in a single space. And Aaron can speak to this better because he tends to have more of these responses, but there has been criticism of the kind of space that's held as being far too one way or the other — not enough of one…I don't know, A1, you have some good examples of this.

Right, while all that's true, the intent is not to be neutral. Not to not acknowledge power dynamics. It's about challenging the overarching narratives that exist, especially around — you know, the veterans aren't the victims of these wars, the people who live under the occupations are — and there's an overwhelming kind of denial of their humanity, and this is ultimately about trying to find different ways of acknowledging their humanity, which is really about acknowledging our own humanity. And there is pushback when people say things that necessarily are — for example, one woman in a performance refused to take a cup, even though she was really interested in the whole performance but in the very end refused to drink out of a cup because it had a name of one of the detainees on it — and she said "Oh, I can't drink out of this. I didn't know it had to do with these terrorists!" And that opened up a space for discussion about and we're not saying, "Oh! We're not going to agree that, oh! Now they're all terrorists because someone said that." It's more a question of, "what informs that? What makes you believe that? Let's look into some of the facts of the situation. And now that you know these facts about how people were detained, how people were extralegally detained, and extraordinarily renditioned, all these layers of how people were brought from over 48 countries around the world to Guantanamo, not just Afghanistan and Iraq, not just individuals who had any kind of relationship to any kind of violent organizations, many who worked with NGO's in Afghanistan, now that that's on the table, now that we've talked about these individuals already —"because a part of the dialogue is about talking about the POW camps that existed in the U.S., Chicago during WWII, which were Nazi POW camps, Italian and German POW camps filled with soldiers, out of those POW camps came love stories, and on Sundays Catholics and Lutherans would go provide Mass and potlucks. So what are the facts that let us humanize in that situation? But we can't even acknowledge the humanity of this supposed enemy today? Why is it that these supposed enemies have to be in Guantanamo and can't be in a POW camp down the road the high school kids can ride their bikes over to and blow kisses to all the young Muslim boys that are in Guantanamo?

And that's a reference to — it seems like almost everywhere that we've spent a significant amount of time and do research, because there are so many POW camps — when we were in Lawrence, Kansas where we were casting the cups, there was a POW camp for primarily Italian soldiers and it turns out they had actually worked in the factory where we were casting, making 15,000 cans of canned vegetables a day to be sent overseas and there was only 1 ordinance in the city of Lawrence during the specific time that the POW camp existed, and that was that there needed to be a boundary and a perimeter around where the camp was, because young girls were coming and blowing kisses to the young POW's. So these stories that are deeply embedded in local culture emerge and provide this connection to this form of tremendously effective kind of "otherizing" in the wars that are happening now and against the people against which they're happening. And so, always trying to bring back the humanity of the actual single, individual people that are affected.

That reminds me of the problem of the Homan facility, this "blacksite" facility we have here in Chicago, which seems to have been weirdly sort of accepted by the public, such that there doesn't seem to have been as much of a public push as there could've been to explicate what's happened with it, with all this discussion of interrogation and rendition connected to that facility. And that's a great jumping-off point

for my next question: what are your thoughts about
the global War on Terror today? It's still happening.
What's different and the same about it in terms of
how it resonates with your project and knowing that
it's propped up on this systemic racism, how do you
go about getting rid of it?

I think the first thing you do in terms of how you
go about getting rid of it is just to acknowledge it.
I don't think that there's any sort of mass acknowl-
edgement that we're at war and that it's this global
war on terror, not specific countries, not specific
people, it's an abstract idea resulting in really a
blanket permission of our state and our military
to really exceed its constitutional powers. The idea
that we're going to win a war based on this abstract
concept is pretty flawed, as seen through the con-
tinuing lack of strategic clarity from the military.

I so agree with Aaron that the first thing is to
just really acknowledge the fact that we're at war
and that there's this sort of this teeter-totter, so
not only bringing to light that this is happen-
ing to families, to communities, to individuals,
not just in this other place. This isn't something
that just happens to terrorists. This happens to
environments, where countries are left without
trees and have 140-degree summers, and then
the flips-side, the other side to the teeter-totter
of that is that we have incredibly anxious young
people who have no funding for their education

because of our military budget. The idea that it's all happening "over there" to this abstract concept, I just absolutely agree with Aaron, first and foremost to acknowledge that we are at war and what does that entail? Taking the time and space to think about what that entails — there just isn't room being made in our lives for that.

> And I think that a lot of communities that are directly affected directly or indirectly by the policies of the global War on Terror and dealing with more of the targeting going on of specific communities, and specifically of the Muslim community, their voices aren't necessarily heard and so part of the project is making sure there's a space where this cross-dialogue between how these wars, how these policies have affected people in their lives on a daily basis for the last decade plus.

And I think there's been a shift in the project in the last maybe 3 years of really recognizing that there's a lot of reason those voices might not want to go public at this time but also that they're not heard. Specifically, for our Links Hall performance, we're really grateful and excited to be collaborating with the Council on Arab-American Relations and with Radio Islam and that this project, where we're bring people together, and where we're bringing together communities that might not otherwise — lots of organizations are working on human rights issues, but may not necessarily have the time or the opportunity to come together and that's what the Saturday night tea engagements are, where we'll have a really diverse kaleidescope of voices from the folks who have done incredible work in Chicago on the John Burge reparations and Black Lives Matter, connecting that with activism and culture that's happening in the Muslim community and connecting the relationships not just between the militarism that's happening there, but in the prison-industrial complex that's happening here and how that affects our communities. But I do think that the lens of thinking about Islamophobia in relationship to the global War on Terror is something that has increased in the project over the last few years.

Deborah Hay [43]

I'm speaking with you on the occasion of your visit
to Chicago to perform at the aMID Festival. What
convinced you to dance at it?

> Well, it's very simple. I love the language, and I
> love the word "amid." And I'm really only think-
> ing about it like a midst, and I love that so much
> that that's what convinced me. When I got the
> invitation I was thinking you know, I haven't really
> performed anywhere but the east coast and the west
> coast in the United States for so long, why would I
> do this? But that language was so attractive to me.

Can you tell me about the work you're presenting?

> It's very stripped down, it's a solo for up to 25
> people and I have no stage needs. In other words,

43   Portions of this interview were originally published at *Newcity*, January 14, 2016,
https://www.newcitystage.com/2016/01/14/unexpected-beauty-michelle-kranicke-be-
be-miller-and-deborah-hay-talk-dance-ageism-and-the-experience-of-socially-con-
scious-performance. An edited version appears here.

it could be performed anywhere, it could be performed in the lobby. It is 10 minutes of performance, and then there's a 10-minute break, and what happens in that ten minute break is really up to whatever happens, and then there's 10 more minutes of performance. And that's it. You know, I'm at a point in my career where it's stripped down to the most minimal and complex, and it's called *my choreographed body*.

You've come out of this background of progressivism and Postmodenism, and I wonder if you think some of the social advances we've seen in recent years such as gay marriage are having an influence in your work?

I don't know much about postmodern thought. All I know is I'm interested in dance engaged in literally with the kind of tension that I bring to the field, and it's a field that is ridden with rules and behaviorism and hierarchies and patterns. My nature, coming out of the sixties in New York what shapes me, is challenging all of these assumptions and there are so many that I'm sure I'll be challenging them until the day I die. So, that's my politics. That's where I can act with political fervor.

Yes, and there is a probable history near work of attempting to move beyond the tangible into a space of preconception, even in situations where I've read view dance work as an embodiment of ideas.

You know, I don't know where that language
comes from.

An earlier, separate interview on your website. It caught my ear, as it were. I'm really curious how you conceive of moving past this notion of perception.

> I feel like the tension in my work has gotten finer and finer as opposed to find in terms of skinnier, and as opposed to bigger, louder, and noisier. The main thing is the dance, like when you read about dance, and when you do dance, we go to the kind of three-dimensional body to look at it in to do it. We're looking at it, we are admiring it and we're questioning what this body can do, and as I get older and as I deepen my interest in the field of dance, I'm not interested in what anybody can do, of course. It's now just so much weaker than what it can do, when you think about the imagination, when you think about singing, what do you think about how we perceive, it's so much bigger than what we can do. And so, that's kind of the evolution of my work.

You know, and I think American culture is very inherently ageist, and I'm wondering how you think your work to help push back against some of that bias?

> Well, they're going to be looking at me. That's all I can say. I mean, I don't know about any of the other work in terms of what the festival's trying

to do, but I think it was brave of them to invite
me. I mean, because, an example would be that I
haven't performed in Chicago since the late 1980s
or 90s. Nobody knows me there in terms of my
work, so I think it's brave of them. You know I
barely work in the United States, most of my work
is in Europe. It was just brave of them to invite me
and in New York, maybe. Because I'm not one of
those traveling around the country and performing
everywhere, my audience is really in Europe and
not in the United States. In New York, maybe.

How do you think the visit informs your own current
work?

So, it gives me a different sense of work, of the
range of work that's going on in dance. I don't
know where I am in relationship to the other art-
ists that are performing there so — I think that
Michelle [Kranicke] putting on a show in the
middle of January in Chicago is pretty radical in
and of itself, so I'd like to support that kind of
challenge to community.

It seems as though there is what has been described
as a second wave of practitioners in the Judson
School mode out there right now and I wonder if you
have been keeping tabs on that and where you think
it stands right now because of the effects of that era
and the influence of your own work on dance. Maybe
it's not even on your radar at this point.

Yeah, it's not even on my radar. You know, I live in Austin, Texas. You have a wonderful festival there called the Fusebox Festival every spring that brings out a lot of talented people. There are an awful lot of young people who are doing interesting work. I just came from from San Francisco, I don't remember the name, but there was a full evening of some very wonderful choreographers. So there is some very good work being done right now in terms of pedagogy and transmission, of what dance can be and how it's beginning to really blossom choreographically. You know choreography is now being taken into more directions than just look at me and look at what I can do, it really is. So there has got to be some good teachers, some good role models for the young people. There's a woman named Heather Kravitz, I really like her work, she was someone who was in this Fusebox Festival. There's a woman in Minneapolis, Karen Sherman who I think is doing some wonderful work and a few others in Minneapolis who are doing some interesting work.

Thanks, it seems like there's some boundary-pushing being done in that vein. I also notice that there's a larger push to incorporate dramaturgy into dance-making. Is that something you're seeing as well?

I can't really answer that one. I can imagine, but I don't really understand it.

Joshua Ishmon [44]

Thanks for sitting down with me today, Joshua. You didn't start out in Chicago, correct?

> I'm originally from Gary, Indiana and started out in dance when I was 7 or 8 — started out in musical theater and West African and took my first ballet class when I was about 12. The company I dance with now, Deeply Rooted Dance Theater (DRDT), the directors had been mentors of mine since I was about 10, so when I graduated high school I was clear that was where I wanted to go. So I danced with their training company a few years and after that I moved up here.

Was this an artistic interest that was rooted in your family history?

> Not at all. My mom was a banker. She worked for Chase before it was Chase, Bank One and

44   Originally published at *Art Intercepts*, June 15, 2017, http://www.artintercepts. org/2017/06/15/movement-matters-an-interview-with-joshua-ishmon.

First Bank of Chicago. She went through all the mergers and worked there 39 years or more. My dad — I honestly don't know what he did when I was a kid. He did department store photography at one point, and then later on became a bus driver. So besides my mom singing occasionally, I didn't have an arts family at all. When I was in elementary school there was a dance troupe that did this West African welcoming dance called Funga, and they came with a little song [sings] funga alafia ashé ashé — and I was so enamored with it. I was like, "I want to do this." So, the following year I joined and that was the first time I got on stage. I was 8. I saw them when I was 7 and joined when I was 7, going into 8. And the first few things we did, they had just started a theater there at the West Side High School and the first musical they were doing was *Joseph and the Technicolor Dream Coat*, the old Donny [Osmond] musical. And so we were doing that and in Funga, what they did was they got the kids to lead it and they said they were going to get one of the kids who was smart to lead it, and I wanted to be that kid. So you yell out "Funga!" and you get to change the set for the rest of them. So, I got it I was so excited that I yelled "Funga!" so hard I lost my voice! So in the middle of it I was wheezing and I couldn't get the word out and just kept on moving.

So, yeah. I was really clear back then about what I wanted to do, and really enjoyed being on stage.

So my parents were very accepting of it up until I
started to look at it as a potential way to make a
living, in addition to the stigma that unfortunately
follows around men in dance.

It does seem to me now that there are a lot more
people pushing back against that.

It's one of those conversations that isn't had, and
at the same time it's hard to have it because of all
the challenges that the homosexual community
goes with to be like, "well, I'm a straight guy in
dance,"…no one cares. Like, I'm a black straight
male in dance. I'm an endangered species, really.
Is there a fight that comes with that? Sure. But no
one cares. It's like, eh. I've got enough challenges
with just being black. I don't need that one.

[laughs] Right? Well, and then, growing up in Gary.
I'm from Indiana too.

Oh okay, what part?

Fort Wayne. Northeast. Our big claim to fame is that
it's where Bruce Nauman was born.

Yeah, it's a place that doesn't really support the arts
all that much. It does and it doesn't at the same
time. Where West Side was this kind of haven for
a lot of the people who wanted to get into theater
or just sing or act in plays they had, everything

happened—they reviewed movies. The director of the guild graduated from my high school and so it kind of started that way, but it became an arts school in '88. It opened in like 1908. Almost literally the day it became an art school, it was on its way to closing. Word on the street was there was like a half million dollars worth of paintings in there that, when they closed the building, they did make sure to take out. It was in 2008 when they closed it and moved [the students] into another school and so now they're in the William A. Wirt High School building. They're in there.

Right, it's tragic and racist how they defund these school systems.

How the government defunds these systems—I've never cared for the manipulation of curriculums. There are so many contributions of people of color that are never spoken about, and I was like, "I don't get why we're not learning about that." Then they're taking the money out of the system to make sure the information is even more limited. That just doesn't make sense to me.

So do you advocate dance as a way to address those problems?

Dance is a way to address it but one thing I always say is I love being an artist because it lets me say whatever the hell I want with little to no context.

You can't lie in art. You can bullshit, but you can't lie. It won't stand up. And the thing about everything else is you can lie, and people will just go along with it. There has to be some truth, some substance even if it's surface, there's just something about it—so that's something I've always enjoyed about the art, you use the vehicle of the art. I run the dance program at Purdue University's Black Cultural Center. So the thing we always say is, "I know you're not here for this. I'm not training you to be a professional dancer." If you do that, fantastic. I'm doing this so you can face things that won't usually get had in academic settings or collegiate settings that people care about their feelings and that's the thing about dance where it can happen in the art. Dancers are brutalized, all the time. It's normally not to their detriment. There's a process around it, like what happens in the ballet world. When you talk about why you got a part or didn't get a part, you get your truth without getting into your feelings about it and then get past that insularity. People are in their own worlds and there are so many environments where they don't have to step outside of it. Even inside of dance, too. There are a lot of people who've only danced in Chicago and only know the Chicago dance scene and as long as they stay in Chicago, they're all good. But the issue I usually have with Chicago, they love stroking their own egos and I'm like, "Ehhh, that thing you just praised was boring. It was incredibly boring!"

Right? There's a lot of that. Too much. But you can't get people to talk about it. They want to talk about ticket sales instead. It's sad. I read the piece you wrote for the *Massachusetts Review* using Charlie Chapman and the *Little Dictator* to talk about the shootings of Philado Castile and Alton Sterling as the basis for your work *When Men...* It was very moving.

> Yeah, this was right after, with those two happening within twelve hours of each other and they hit me so hard and I couldn't tell you why. Probably, with all the things I've seen in my life, being from Gary and all that, seeing that video of when Philado Castile was dying — it was on live Facebook. His daughter was in the backseat — all the things that went wrong in it and all the people trying to justify it and probably the most comforting thing, right before I started making that piece, there's a party that happens called Party Noire that takes place at the Promontory in Hyde Park. Beautiful place run by three beautiful, wonderful women. I remember walking in there, I remember thinking I had to get out and go somewhere with some good energy because I got to get out the house. And I walked in and it was so evident that was the reason that everyone was there because the whole community, at least as far as I could see, they all got hit by that. It was almost cathartic, it was healing for all of us to be in that space. I remember [after that], walking into the studio, and I turned

on the music and 3 hours later, *When Men…* was done and every day was like that. I didn't have any words to say, we were just doing it.

Carole McCurdy [45]

You're from the north side of Chicago.

Yes, I grew up in East Rogers Park, and that's where I live now. I love it because the lake's at my doorstep. I swam practically every day in August! I lived in New York City from 1984 to 2003, moved back to take care of my mother just before she died, and ended up staying here. I have a fond nostalgia for my days in the East Village and miss my East Coast friends, but Chicago offered me life-changing opportunities that have been so gratifying. I can't imagine leaving it anytime soon. Well, except for the winter, when I'll head to South America.

How did you initially get interested in dance? As an artist or in terms of doing it professionally?

Through social dancing. Almost twenty years ago

45   Originally published at Sixty Inches From Center, Dec. 29, 2016, http://sixtyinches-fromcenter.org/movement-matters-carole-mccurdy.

I fell into the embrace of Argentine tango, and it thrilled and challenged me on so many levels. You're creating a circle with a partner and a circular path through time and space, and every time you go around the dance floor it's "same-same but different." It's infused with nostalgia but also totally immediate, improvised moment by moment. Over the years I've spent many months in Buenos Aires tracing those circles. Before tango, I was hunched over manuscripts, working as a copy editor for book publishers in New York, lost in my head and with all kinds of crunk in my neck and shoulders. For a geek like me, dancing in the structured environment of tango was a great way to reenter the physical world. Humbling and humiliating at times, but it slowly turned me into a maker through movement. I started exploring butoh about twelve years ago, and it jolted me into ways of thinking about embodiment that went beyond social constructs and into the primal and metaphysical. I learned that physical limitations (well, I guess I'm talking about my own not-so-neurotypical movement traits) could be mined as an asset artistically. I started performing and making pieces, and eventually had to start calling myself an artist. That took some getting used to.

Who were the people that most influenced your work in dance?

I took my first butoh classes with Nicole LeGette in Chicago after moving back here from New York, and I imprinted on her like a duckling. In less than a year she had me performing in her pieces. That gave me so much — the confidence to work through the challenges she set, examples of processes for composing work, and in those classes and ensemble pieces I met so many people that I continue to collaborate with and learn from. [They're] the artistic friendships that make my world. Having a teacher and mentor who was younger than me was a lucky way to get started. While getting a lot of rigorous training, I could watch Nicole's artistic ideas ripening, and that gave me courage to start developing my own ideas and follow my own instincts. Improvising on solo pieces, often at one-time underground events, gave me the chance to experiment and develop a sense of myself as a performer. Now I'm working on a project where I'm aiming for the rigor and contrariness of butoh while taking inspiration from the partner dynamics of tango. It's crazy. We'll see [how it goes].

Describe where you'd like to go with your work from here.

If I could use sentences to articulate the things I want to project into the audience, I'd be writing essays and not dancing. Saying that is not only a dancerly dodge, but very much in the tradition of butoh, a form that arose in Japan after WWII in a time of shock, mourning, and cultural protest. One of the hallmarks of butoh, which has has branched out beyond Japan as a dance subculture, is that it constantly recontextualizes itself, always challenging our understandings of the body in time and space. When it works, the effect is uncanny and transformative. When it fails, it's merely maudlin or comical. I'm proud of my sad and amusing failures, for sure, but I hope that some moments of my butoh-influenced work have messed with somebody's head.

Carole McCurdy. Image by John Sisson.

How do you think what you're working on now in
your residency at High Concept Labs and elsewhere
will change what you're doing?

> My new project, *Waver*, is still early gestating and
> although I'm working with influences from butoh and
> tango, the result probably won't feel quite like either.
> Nor do I want to make a hybrid. A strange beast with
> hints of the familiar: that would satisfy me.

What do you feel like have been your most successful
artistic aspirations?

> Maybe it's perverse, but I'd rather not dwell on aspi-
> rations. For initiating anything, they're necessary,
> but then you start working and everything's real
> and grounded and honestly unwieldy. Performances
> that worked best for me have come from "embrace
> the accident." For example, I recently did a solo
> improvisation piece at New Room, an informal
> event curated by April Noga and Eli Halpern: it
> was barely rehearsed and involved a wig that con-
> cealed my face. When I tried it at home I could
> see through the wig well enough, I thought. At
> the performance I couldn't see anything and had
> to feel my way around: a wonderful vulnerability
> and new information to play with. I was delighted
> to build on it, and it literally connected me with
> the audience. Yes! But what I'm starting to learn
> to avoid (and it's a mistake I've made a few times)
> is overloading a piece with too many elements. I

have to resist the oversolicitous tendency to dump
out the box and share every toy.

As an artist who is a late bloomer to dance, what
do you feel are the resistances you face in our often
ageist culture?

Ha, I was just thinking about having used the
word nostalgia twice already here. Dance is made
by the body in space and time, and as someone
who started performing and making dance after
the age of forty I've gotten to offer a fresh perspec-
tive on that. One of the simple movement scores
I revisit is a thing I call Slow Hurry. Struggling
with time is the one place I've always been. My
friends know I'm usually late for appointments,
and they suffer with me. It's a moral failure or a
social abuse, I guess, but until I'm rehabilitated the
inexact connection fascinates me. Stepping onto
the stage late means "doing it wrong" in a way that
opens a new frame. Some of my pieces have looked
overtly at aging, illness, and mortality (after treat-
ment for two kinds of cancer, that became a part
of my material). I could make a conscious effort
to stick to those subjects, but I think I can count
on them to be present while I look at other things!
Fortunately my training is in two dance fields that
revere the aging dancer and work with time in
complex ways. In Buenos Aires there are ninety-
year-olds out on the dance floor showing young
tangueros how it's done. And Kazuo Ohno, who

along with Tatsumi Hijikata brought butoh into the world, danced until he died at 103. No question that American dominant culture values youth over age, but here's a late bloomer who found audience and support thanks to Links Hall, Chicago Dancemakers Forum, High Concept Labs, and a bunch of young artists out of SAIC. Whoa: dance as a survivor institution quite generously offered space for me. But outside of music videos, dance itself is as marginalized as a "sweet little old lady." So where I see the need to push back and find change is at the level of dominant culture. One way I can help make those changes happen: keep dancing.

Kiam Marcello Junio [46]

You spent most of your childhood outside the States,
correct?

> I'm from the Philippines. I lived there, grew up
> there, and then moved to Japan when I was 10.
> I was adopted into my aunt's family whose hus-
> band was in the Navy, and kind of grew up in this
> really international U.S. military community in
> Japan and then moved to California when I was
> 16. From there I did other things, and joined the
> Navy for 7 years.

Do you have an artistic family?

> There are a lot of musicians in my family, but not
> necessarily visual artists. Pianists. Tuba. All kinds
> of everything really. A lot of pianists. But it was
> always a thing that you do on the side. I have one
> uncle who was a traveling musician, so he was kind

46   Originally published at *Art Intercepts*, July 15, 2017, http://www.artintercepts.
org/2017/07/15/movement-matters-an-interview-with-kiam-marcelo-juno.

of an influence a little bit, but my parents never encouraged me to do art; it was something I had to pursue on my own. When I joined the Navy at 19, I was prepared to turn that into a lifelong career. I thought I would go into the medical field afterward. I was working as a hospital corpsman, I think they called it. Even when I was in the military and doing all of that, every time I had free time, I was always making art whether I was doing photography or making collage or some other thing — mostly photography.

Were you deployed then, too?

I was deployed a few times on TD — temporary duty — but I was never in a war zone. I was down range but I pursued photography while I was in the military. It was a very accessible media, where I could really immerse myself in it and learn about the past while distinguishing between myself and the audience which I felt like worked for me as a bit of a shield. Photography, at that time, was becoming more and more — not pedestrian — but more colloquial in a way. More and more people were getting into photography as a kind of daily activity, before cell phones. When the iPhone came out was about the middle of my Navy career. So photography really gave me this platform to understand art-making and how to approach it in different ways but still have people around. So when I got out of the Navy—and I got out because

I knew I was an artist and knew I had to pursue this field or I was not going to be happy — I left and the only school I applied to was The School of the Art Institute of Chicago because they gave me a scholarship. It was like: "Oh, I love Chicago." I had done bootcamp just north of here, and my initial medical training was in Great Lakes. So when I was in medical training I'd come down to Chicago every other weekend or so and just come down by myself, go to events, and just be by myself and very independent, away from the military. So I took that feeling with me and I knew Chicago would be a good place to come back to and start over.

So Chicago and SAIC was formative for you.

In my first year at SAIC I was in photography, but I wasn't doing a lot of photo work. I was doing mostly installation and video. And then outside of school I started taking burlesque classes at Vaudezilla and I was really intrigued by performance. I've always been a dancer and performer, really. An actor, vocalist — I was in a choir for years — a lot of other things but, again, performing really comes naturally to me and I knew that I wanted to see what it looked like in an art context away from theatre and away from the stage. SAIC has a really great performance community. I met a lot of people there who helped show me how to account for ideas in bodily movement, or create a space by inhabiting a space.

It's interesting how you were translating one art form into another.

Yes, it was a progression from a flat image, from 3D reality into an image and then the flat image became another 3D space and then I realized the 3D space was one I was embodying and it was a translation of the "where is the art?" question, right? Is it the thing that you're photographing, or is it you, the performer, who creates that image, or is it in the experience with the audience? I'm understanding how all of these different lenses operate and how they create the art in multiple layers. And I think early on I understood how my personal body is also a political body, is also a sensual body, is also a spiritual body. After leaving the military but before coming to Chicago, I took a yoga training course. It was a 1-month long residency that really delved into yoga philosophy and that really influenced how I was thinking about all of these layers I was perceiving. Then, applying that to art-making felt really natural to me. I didn't really realize until I was in school and saw the lack of representation of Filipino artists, and the Filipino-American experience — the intersection of that with being a veteran and thinking about those in terms of gender and coming into myself as a queer person.

Yes, and especially with that background as a queer
person in the military.

> Yes, and my response to it back then was a sense
> of camouflaging, playing the role of being quiet
> and doing my job, which is what my visual art is
> really rooted in was the experience of having to
> camouflage myself in hyper-masculine society. So,
> I think performance art, beginning in burlesque
> and then transforming into drag, was for me a way
> to take these identifiers that I wasn't supposed to
> have or that I was supposed to work out of myself
> — like being feminine, speaking with an accent —
> I identify as femme and queer, trans in the larger
> umbrella sense of it, in the way I think people are
> familiar with it. I'm gender nonconforming.

So, there's this whole shift then in your earlier per-
formance work I've seen, to bring performance into
installation, making responses, for instance, to Felix
Gonzalez-Torres.

> Yeah, I think definitely in the beginning.

Taking that and articulating it into a whole other
sense of what your voice is out there.

> My own agency in my work and in these spaces
> is always changing. In the last few years it's
> been really interesting how people have taken
> note of what I'm doing and have really begun to

understand where I'm coming from. That's really encouraging and really beautiful and helped me to push even further and delve even deeper into where these ideas are coming from.

Kerry James Marshall [47]

Morning outside Kerry James Marshall's studio at 39th and Indiana. The gently sunlit streets are empty except for a small coterie of people waiting for a bus. A liquor store, beauty shops and churches are within view. Birds flutter overhead. Trees. Street signs, pavement and trash. Vacant lots. Car engines ricochet off the rows of one-story buildings down the block, sound peaking for an instant before disappearing back into stillness. Music plays just beyond earshot. "Been that way for decades," Marshall will tell you.

His painting *7 am Sunday Morning* offers a nearly life-sized perspective of this street scene. A perfect surface uninterrupted by evidence of a brushstroke spreads out across the reality, almost rising up from within the buildings, the grass, the ironworks. These one-story buildings, this watery blue expanse of sky, a Robert Taylor home in the distance, sheet music for gospel and soul tunes including *What's Goin' On* and Crossroads Blues dance out into thin air. On the far right of the image, a beam of light streams down through the railing past a water tower — yet, something's not quite

47   Originally published in *Newcity*, October 26, 2013, https://art.newcity.com/2003/10/16/marshall-art-exploring-the-new-black-aesthetic-with-kerry-james-marshall.

right. Behind and within the refracted light, the hazy outline of a building emerges. Atop that building sits the water tower through which the refracted sunlight flows but, in reality, neither building nor water tower actually exist. Though they appear here on the canvas, these structures represent an extradimensional world revealed only in the instant depicted on the canvas. Marshall refers to that light as "a blinded space where hallucinations can occur," a place imagined into existence from the view outside his studio.

Inside his studio, shelves are filled with cans of Campbell's soup. On another shelf across the room, white and red thermoses are stacked one atop the other. A bouquet of blue, orange and yellow flowers sits on a table in a far corner of the back room. A sign from the 16th Street Baptist Church, a collection of Kabuki dolls. Bottles of Tylenol fill the corner of a desk; four toy firemen's badges still in plastic hang on the wall. Amidst such evidence of the long stretches of time spent here, a row of huge black granite sculptures, draped in plastic drip covers, solemnly loom, ready for shipment: these are the artist's Cubist renderings of the continent of Africa.

A full-time professor of art for the past eight years at the University of Illinois at Chicago, Marshall is a reserved and calm man who dotes on questions asked of him. His upcoming solo exhibition at the Museum of Contemporary Art, *One True Thing: Meditations on Black Aesthetics*, encompasses worlds torn between cultural traditions. "I wanted to really look at what that means, to demonstrate what a black aesthetic is," says Marshall, who cites the heavily patterned work that came out of the Black Arts Movement (or BAM) of the seventies as a point of departure, including the recurrent Egyptian pyramidal design. "To work with an elliptical set of references in which everything refers to being black, that takes the idea of being black for granted, images that are relatively prosaic or mundane, and then let the evocation of black aesthetics seep out," Marshall explains. Among the sources Marshall employs are ancient African mythological figures, including a Congo nail fetish, called a Nkisi, sometimes adorned with tiny stomach chambers inside of which are stored magical substances. Most documented statues resemble porcupines since, when believers had a wish they wanted to fulfill, they would drive a nail into the small figurine. "When you drive the nail in, that secures your request," says Marshall. "And Nkisi get their power from repeated use."

Marshall's repertory of ancient gods include Senuto — executioner figures, with long, pole-like arms. "They used these in trials, moving the long arms to point out the guilty. And the Boli were from Mali," says Marshall, pointing out the black-and-white photograph of a large, stone-like figure with no eyes or ears that resembles a buffalo. Boli figures were ritual objects that were often buried. "A mysterious figure, like an animal. Boli were transitional, they escorted people from the material to the spiritual world." A host of others follow: Elsiji figures were replacements for a dead twin. Oba figures from Benine were warrior king figures, often appearing in bronze casts posed with a sword. Marshall has sculpted each figure as a study, making a Senuto for instance, out of cloth sacks and twine.

Rifling through a stack of papers, Marshall takes out a panel from the comic-strip art that will also appear in his MCA show, a fully colored image depicting a Nkisi, Senuto, Elsiji and Oba darting through the panel like a team of superheroes rushing into battle. To the far left, a Boli, large as a meteor, floats into the frame. Marshall pulls out another sheet, this one depicting a night scene in a museum, security guards gazing confusedly as they wander through a whole room of display cases with their glass frames broken out. "They escaped from the museum, actually the African wing at the Art Institute," says Marshall. "In a sense, they've escaped."

Every day Marshall reads the funnies in the Tribune. "I was a big Peanuts fan," Marshall says of his comic-art influences. "I used to read *Doonesbury, Non Sequitur, Dilbert, The Boondocks,* and I noticed how infrequently a strip by a black artist was getting syndicated. Something like *Where We At?* didn't really take off. That strip ran for a little while, but it wasn't really clever. It was kind of a black version of *Sally Forth.* Certainly, it wasn't controversial."

He often takes the news as his subject matter. One sequence of panels that forms a central part of the story in his MCA show examines the CHA demolition that precipitated the relocation of tenants from Stateway Gardens projects at 37th and State as the second of "two great migrations" experienced by the black population in Chicago. "The people are refusing to leave because they think the whole thing's unfair," Marshall explains of these often chaotic and sometimes violent scenes, pointing to a series of panels that lead up to a panorama of buildings and streets drawn to resemble a commercial for a moving company. In another series of five panels, Marshall has rendered a figure from several different views, as if seen from five different camera angles. The phrase "Everything will be alright, I just know it will" appears repeatedly in several different panels as the displacement of the main characters in the CHA drama continues apace.

Finishing his comics requires that his drawn-and-inked pages be transferred onto newsprint, to more closely resemble strips in daily papers. "That also allows me to position them all over the page," says Marshall. "If it all comes off correctly, there will be three or four stories that all connect to make an epic story, like it was released episodically. The whole thing starts somewhere in the middle, kind of like the 'Star Wars' trilogy started in the middle of the story." Besides including the Rhythm Master comics he produced for the 2000 Carnegie International exhibition, Marshall has produced eighteen new sections, often with multiple panels, some with three frames.

Another key section in Marshall's series of comic art depicts a townhouse with a sign in the front lawn: "The Ancient Egyptian Museum." "This character encounters a man here who teaches him his African powers," Marshall explains. "This was a real place, and there are Afrocentric scholars who discuss mystery systems; Kismet, come down out of African Egypt, that show how black people were integral to the rise of Egypt. But this little townhouse — that's how this happens, you inadvertently stumble on this source of information. It's a source of tension in the black community on some level, the spiritual differences between black and European traditions."

In those spiritual differences Marshall finds a major perceptual schism, a cultural inability to see or not see what's present. "It's a metaphysical idea. I'm interested in what happens in that space of between perceptions." Nothing conveys this more powerfully than *Black Painting*, a night scene that, upon first seeing it, stunts the viewer's vision with the sheer density of its blackness. Upon sustained viewing, however, shapes slowly emerge, black-on-black, until coalescing to form indiscernible abstract representations, then solid geometries and finally a bedroom scene. A man sleeps in a dim moonlit room, his black panther lamp curled up in a subtle, enchanting reference to the subject matter of a black unconscious soon to awaken.

About the Author

Workman's work centers on analyzing and theorizing the outgrowth of new artistic forms in response to antagonism by systems and structures of inequality, and their sources in the socio-cultural forces that drive, legitimize and continuously perpetuate them throughout ancient history and into the modern age. To date, this includes books with Golden Spike and StepSister Presses, and bylines with newspapers, magazines and other media including the Chicago Tribune, Guardian US, Newcity magazine, as a columnist at Art Intercepts and WBEZ Chicago Public Radio. Throughout, he has consistently sought to give voice to the underrepresented and marginalized, whether preferencing LGBTQ and people of color, or others whose own life and work are shaped by these forces of inequality.

Often, his analysis of these structural biases reveals the influence of what urban planners refer to as "place identity," a factor intrinsic to the background socio-cultural issues of the art, performance and dances that are his main subjects.

As a writer, the perspectival shifts that thusly take place in the gap between these distinct concerns also constitute a zone of influence between writing, dance and contemporary art. Each overlap in definitions of art as made by living artists, whose perspectives are in some ways formed by the complexities of their place in a historical moment. In recent years, this has led him to a wider concern with the language-based, instructive aspects of choreography, and how its sociological dimensions may meaningfully be utilized to model precepts of equal treatment through movement-based social interactions.